ERASMUS

JON BANSTEAK
07985 834725
+1-267-344-7857
TUE 13 OCT 2008
Fee 13 OCT 2008 - 22f

OUTSTANDING CHRISTIAN THINKERS

Series Editor: Brian Davies OP, Professor of Philosophy at Fordham University, New York.

The Cappadocians
Anthony Meredith SJ

Augustine
Mary T. Clark RSCJ

Catherine of Siena
Giuliana Cavallini OP

Kierkegaard
Julia Watkin

Lonergan
Frederick Rowe SJ

Reinhold Niebuhr
Kenneth Durkin

Venerable Bede
Benedicta Ward SLG

The Apostolic Fathers
Simon Tugwell OP

Denys the Areopagite
Andrew Louth

Calvin
T. H. L. Parker

Erasmus
Erika Rummel

Hans Urs von Balthasar
John O'Donnell SJ

Teresa of Avila
Archbishop Rowan Williams

Bultmann
David Fergusson

Karl Barth
John Webster

Aquinas
Brian Davies OP

Paul Tillich
John Heywood Thomas

Karl Rahner
William V. Dych SJ

Anselm
G. R. Evans

Newman
Avery Cardinal Dulles SJ

Bonhoeffer
Stephen Plant

ERASMUS

Erika Rummel

continuum
LONDON • NEW YORK

CONTINUUM

The Tower Building, 11 York Road, London SE1 7NX
15 East 26th Street, New York NY 10010

www.continuumbooks.com

First published 2004

British Library Cataloguing-in-Publication Data
A catalogue record for this book is available from the British Library.

ISBN: 0-8264-6813-6 (hardback)
0-8264-6814-4 (paperback)

Typeset by Kenneth Burnley, Wirral, Cheshire
Printed and bound in Great Britain by Cromwell Press Ltd, Trowbridge, Wilts

Contents

Editorial Foreword

St Anselm of Canterbury (1033–1109) once described himself as someone with faith seeking understanding. In words addressed to God he says 'I long to understand in some degree thy truth, which my heart believes and loves. For I do not seek to understand that I may believe, but believe in order to understand.'

This is what Christians have always inevitably said, either explicitly or implicitly. Christianity rests on faith, but it also has content. It teaches and proclaims a distinctive and challenging view of reality. It naturally encouarges reflection. It is something to think about; something about which one might even have second thoughts.

But what have the greatest Christian thinkers said? And is it worth saying? Does it engage with modern problems? Does it provide us with a vision to live by? Does it make sense? Can it be preached? Is it believable?

The Outstanding Christian Thinkers series is offered to readers with questions like these in mind. It aims to provide clear, authoritative and critical accounts of outstanding Christian writers, from New Testament times to the present. It ranges across the full spectrum of Christian thought to include Catholic and Protestant thinkers, thinkers from East and West, thinkers ancient, medieval and modern.

The series draws on the best scholarship currently available, so it will interest all with a professional concern for the history of Christian ideas. But contributors also write for general readers who have little or no previous knowledge of the subjects to be dealt with. Its volumes should therefore prove helpful at a popular as well as an academic level. For the most part they are devoted to a single thinker, but occasionally the subject is a movement or school of thought.

BRIAN DAVIES OP

Preface

A book on Erasmus's thought must begin with a caveat: Erasmus had a philosophical bent, but he was no systematic philosopher. His writings contain inconsistencies and ambiguities, some of them rooted in literary conventions. It is clearly unrealistic to look for perfect consistency in an oeuvre that includes fiction and rhetorical exercises. But even if we limit ourselves to his essays and other works of non-fiction, we find variants and deviations from the mainstream of his thought. Context is therefore of paramount importance in interpreting Erasmus's meaning. Some of the inconsistencies may indicate a natural shifting of opinion over time, others a careful husbanding of the truth resulting in adjusting the message to the intended audience. For example, criticism of the Catholic Church voiced after 1521, when Luther became anathema, has graver implications than criticism dating from pre-Reformation times. Likewise, statements made in a personal letter carry more weight than those found in a declamation or put in the mouth of a fictitious character. Erasmus had occasion to complain of readers who failed to make these distinctions. When critics cited the dialogues in his *Colloquia* to prove Erasmus's heterodoxy, he scoffed that they would declare him an infidel if he introduced a Turk as speaker. Similarly, he lectured a critic who was offended by a declamation in praise of marriage: 'Whoever professes to give a declamation disclaims all responsibility for the opinions stated.'[1] In the same vein, Erasmus complained of anachronistic interpretations that discovered 'Lutheran' thought in writings published before the reformer came to prominence. Such historical and literary considerations are fundamental to an understanding of Erasmus's motives and state of mind. In other words, writing about Erasmus's thought means writing a *biographie raisonnée*. My book, then, is arranged chronologically, following

Erasmus's physical and mental progression and focusing successively on literature and education, piety, political thought, biblical scholarship and theological controversy.

The first, introductory chapter provides general background. It supplies information on Erasmus's life and works, based on a critical examination of two important autobiographical documents: the *Compendium vitae* and the *Catalogus*. The second chapter deals with a cluster of works written in the 1490s and early 1500s, which communicate the essential features of his educational philosophy. They are apparent in the teaching aids he published in his early career: a Greek grammar, a handbook of Latin style, anthologies of proverbs, similes and historical anecdotes, a manual of letter-writing and dialogues servings as models of conversational Latin. His pedagogical thought is summed up in several tracts: a curriculum proposal, a short treatise on manners, and two works explaining his theory of education, one for boys in general, the other addressed to theology students. Comparing these early works with late publications such as the *Ciceronianus* or *Ecclesiastes* evinces the continuity of certain ideas. Throughout his life, Erasmus shared the anthropological optimism characteristic of Renaissance humanists, believing in the capacity of human beings to improve themselves through education. While he recognized that success depended on three factors – nature, instruction and practice – he consistently placed a heavy responsibility on parents and teachers, and was inclined to attribute a student's inability to benefit from instruction to parental neglect or inadequate teaching methods. Although he placed the traditional emphasis on imitation, he defined it in a more comprehensive sense as a process of creative appropriation. His remarks on teaching methods reflect a new sensitivity typical of humanistic manuals, which emphasize a cordial relationship between teacher and student and counsel the teacher to adapt his material to the understanding and talents of the student. Erasmus's main pedagogical work, *De pueris instituendis*, echoes earlier humanistic treatises on the goals of education in combining intellectual with moral training and stressing its civic dimension.

Erasmus's curriculum proposals may be read as manifestos of humanism. They contain the features that epitomize Renaissance humanism: an admiration for classical antiquity, an inclination to cite classical sources in preference to medieval writings and an emphasis on language studies, rhetoric and social sciences in preference to logic. It must be stressed, however, that Erasmus did not promote a purely secular humanism. The answer to the question raised in the *Ciceronianus*: 'Shall we Christians before other Christians [speak] as the pagan Cicero did before pagans?' could not be answered with a simple yes or no. Instead, Erasmus recommended the rhetorical virtue of *aptum*: appropriateness. It was not impossible to be both a Christian and a Ciceronian. After all, *imitatio* did not consist in aping Cicero's vocabulary and sentence structure, but in speaking, like Cicero, clearly, forcefully and *appropriately*. It was fitting therefore that the Christian humanist should speak with Ciceronian eloquence but at the same time breathe the spirit of Christ.[2]

Chapter 3 deals with Erasmus's concept of piety in the personal and public sphere. In the *Enchiridium militis Christiani* Erasmus fused Pauline with patristic concepts. He saw piety as the culmination of a progression from physical to spiritual things. He did not reject ceremonies out of hand, but regarded them as crutches supporting the weaker brethren in their journey toward a more perfect piety independent of rites. Yet piety had a practical dimension in the sense that it left its imprint on the life of the faithful. This living faith, or *philosophia Christi*, was predicated on ardent love rather than cold routine. Erasmus explicitly connected the *Enchiridium* with his famous *jeu d'ésprit*, the *Encomium moriae*, explaining that it presented in witty fashion what he had expressed in a serious vein in the earlier work. Dame Folly's speech concludes on the same note as the *Enchiridium*. True human happiness, she explains, requires a kind of heavenly folly, that is, the placing of spiritual above material things – priorities that the world regards as foolish.

In his writings Erasmus frequently adverts to the relationship between piety and learning. In his view piety was the antithesis of academic theology, which he condemned as *curiositas*: vain speculation on matters that transcend human understanding. At the same time he protested against those who would equate piety with ignorance. *Docta pietas*, a learned piety that knows its limits, was his ideal, and Saint Jerome was the man who embodied it. Piety also had a civic dimension for Erasmus. It denoted moral integrity in social relations. Christian morality becomes the defining element of public and private conduct and is thus at the heart of Erasmus's political philosophy.

Chapter 4 focuses on three aspects of Erasmus's political thought that are prominent in his works: the notion of a hierarchical order; the politics of war and peace; and the relationship between state and Church. The heavenly and earthly realms are linked in an image Erasmus adopted in the *Enchiridium*. He depicted Christ surrounded by clergy, princes and common people in three concentric circles. The iconography, which parallels a traditional feudal image, assigns to Christ a position analogous to that of the king, who delegates his powers to the lower estates. The image creates a hierarchical order. The ideal ruler is a father-figure representing God, dispensing justice and providing spiritual leadership. As God's steward on earth, he must give an account of his actions in heaven. The decision to go to war requires a careful analysis of motives and weighing of the alternatives. Although Erasmus accepted the concept of 'just war', he prefers spiritual weapons to battle-gear. Peace and consensus are prominent themes in his writings. In *Dulce bellum inexpertis* and *Querela pacis* he deplored the destructive and dehumanizing effects of warfare. His emphasis on concord, however, has epistemological implications as well (see Chapter 6). Describing the respective roles of secular and ecclesiastical rulers, Erasmus discerned a parallel purpose but calls for different modes of action. Both authorities are concerned with the welfare of the people, but the princes of the Church lead through preaching and teaching; the secular princes dispense justice and maintain order. If they fulfil their respective duties, the spiritual as well as the material welfare of the people is assured.

Erasmus's biblical scholarship and the polemics it engendered is the subject of Chapter 5. In his curriculum outline for students of theology he emphasized the importance of returning to the source text: the Bible. The Word of God was inherently rhetorical. Its persuasive quality allowed the divine message to enter the human heart. Unlike traditional academic theology with its focus on logic, biblical studies evoked in the adept a 'zeal for the true religion of the Gospel'.[3] The acquisition of philological and rhetorical skills permitted students to examine the texts in the original language and to make use of the mediating function of language to draw nearer to God.

Although Erasmus did not develop a philosophy of language, he repeatedly made a connection between speaking and thinking correctly, noting in the prolegomena to his New Testament edition that speech is made up of words (which he relates to body) and meaning (which he relates to soul). As a philologist, he believed that an understanding of the literal meaning of the Bible must precede moral and doctrinal exegesis. He acknowledged theology as the 'queen' of sciences, but claimed for philology the role of 'handmaid'. In his edition of the New Testament, he attempted to provide the basis for a theological exegesis by supplying a correct text and translation. The edition involved him in numerous controversies with Catholic theologians who questioned his qualifications for undertaking the task and accused him of blasphemy for correcting the apostles and Jerome, then widely regarded as the author of the Vulgate translation. Soon more serious accusations were launched against Erasmus, as critics of the edition began to scrutinize his annotations for heterodox interpretations. The Paris theologian Noël Béda undertook a similar critique of Erasmus's *Paraphrases* of the New Testament, pointing out what he perceived as parallels between Erasmus's and Luther's teachings. Erasmus vigorously protested these accusations in apologiae directed against his critics, but could not prevent an investigation of his works by a commission of Spanish theologians in 1527 and by the faculty of theology at Paris, which in 1531 issued a formal condemnation of certain passages in his works.

The controversies between Erasmus and the theologians were a facet of the humanist–scholastic debate, then at its height in northern universities. Biblical humanists and theologians confronted each other over a number of issues: academic qualifications, curriculum and teaching authority. The theologians insisted that an academic degree was a necessary prerequisite for dealing competently with the biblical text; humanists regarded philological training as the principal qualification. A degree in theology was predicated on the study of logic; humanists urged the inclusion of language studies. Theologians jealously guarded their exclusive right to interpret the Bible; humanists insisted that an authoritative interpretation was impossible without the philological skills necessary for an understanding of the literal meaning. In the 1520s the debate became entangled in the Reformation controversy, as theologians accused biblical humanists of having paved the way for Lutheranism. Erasmus, who was regarded as the leading humanist in Northern Europe, became a prime target for attacks by scholastic theologians.

Chapter 6 takes up the thread at this point, investigating the accusation that 'Erasmus laid the egg, and Luther hatched it.' While Erasmus was a caustic critic of Church abuses, he never challenged Catholic doctrine. He was initially sympathetic toward Luther, but withdrew his support from the reformers when the movement became schismatic. His satirical criticism of popular superstition and the commercialization of religion may have furnished the reformers with ammunition; his critical edition of the New Testament may have supplied the raw material for their interpretations; and the counsel he tendered to princes and prelates may have resembled their proposals. Unlike the reformers, however, Erasmus did not deny the teaching authority of the Church and never subscribed to the central Reformation principle of *sola scriptura*. He respected the traditions of the Church and advocated a house-cleaning rather than a systemic change. His rejection of the Reformation movement was predicated on epistemological considerations as well. His polemic with Luther over free will pinpoints the essential disagreement between the two men. Luther believed in the clarity of Scripture; Erasmus denied it. Luther rightly labelled Erasmus a sceptic, but it is important to understand that he was no sceptic in the classical sense of the word. The Pyrrhonists and Academic sceptics of the ancient world suspended judgement in the absence of a rational solution to a problem. Erasmus, the 'Christian sceptic', used consensus as a decision-making tool. In Erasmus's view the authoritative teachings of the Church represented the consensus of the faithful reached over the centuries and confirmed by God, who would not let his Church go astray. Thus Erasmus's scepticism was an aspect of Christian humanism in the sense that he adapted classical ideas to Christian exigencies.

It was Erasmus's misfortune to live at a time of strife, when partisan spirit was valued more highly than intellectual doubt and when commitment was in greater demand than tolerance. The historian Roland Bainton has rightly pointed out that Erasmus never received his due because 'he founded no church to perpetuate his memory'[4] and, one might add, no philosophical school to perpetuate his Christian scepticism. Within two decades of his death, the Catholic Church had proscribed his writings. Even in Protestant countries, Erasmus was eventually reduced from a religious thinker to a style model, and the term 'Erasmian' came to denote a writer who exemplified Erasmus's rhetorical skills. His reputation as a champion of peace was more enduring. Pacifists then and now tend to cite Erasmus in support of their ideas, but they are Erasmians only in the broadest sense of the word. Their pleas are generally based on humanitarian or religious grounds, while Erasmus's irenicism had an epistemological basis. Erasmus himself would not have complained about his failure to attract partisans or create an Erasmian party. In fact, he disparaged party labels and declared that he 'would be neither a leader nor an adherent of a sect'. It was enough for him to be called a Christian.[5]

1

'Read this by yourself and in secret': Erasmus constructs his Life

In 1524 Conradus Goclenius, a Latin professor at Louvain, received a message from his old mentor, Desiderius Erasmus of Rotterdam. The letter was delivered by a personal messenger and began with a warning, written in Greek: 'Read this by yourself and in secret.'[1] The cautionary words were necessary because letters of famous men were a highly valued commodity, and the proud recipients were likely to share their treasure immediately with friends and neighbours. Some letters never reached their destination. They were intercepted and sold to printers. 'Everything is opened on the way', Erasmus complained. 'Even the secretaries who write out our letters make copies available to the public.'[2] The letter to Goclenius contained information that was for his eyes alone.

Erasmus was almost 60 years old, old enough 'to prepare for the judgement of God'.[3] He had been ailing for some time and had had premonitions of death. 'There remains the last act of this drama', he wrote to Goclenius, 'and to play out my part in it I need a friend, someone like you.'[4] The packet he sent contained, in addition to the letter, money to be disbursed to friends after Erasmus's death and to Goclenius himself, who was to oversee the publication of Erasmus's *Opera omnia*. Such editions were usually prefaced with a Life of the author. The biographer's task was sensitive, too sensitive apparently to be entrusted to others. No one could paint a better literary portrait of Erasmus than Erasmus himself. He therefore enclosed an autobiographical sketch for Goclenius' guidance.[5] Now known by the title *Compendium vitae* (Brief Life), the sketch was written in the third person to give it an air of detachment. There are of course well known historical precedents for this practice. Authors from Julius Caesar to Pope Pius II wrote autobiographical accounts in the third person to ensure that posterity heard their side of the story.

Erasmus promised to tell 'the whole story'[6] but, as is to be expected, the *Compendium* contains a tightly edited narrative. Until the publication of the *Adages* (1500), a collection of classical proverbs that became Erasmus's ticket of admission to the circle of humanists, his life had been full of embarrassments, compromises and inglorious incidents that might tarnish the lustre of his reputation unless presented in the right light. In the sketch he sent to Goclenius, and in other autobiographical narratives, Erasmus attempted to transform these unpleasant experiences into picaresque tales. He romanticized his illegitimate birth; he satirized his opponents; he sensationalized sordid details. In a word, he approached biography like fiction: developing a plot-line, strewing the narrative with dialogue and weaving in amusing and paradigmatic anecdotes. In these autobiographical accounts, Erasmus appears variously as an amiable character among admiring friends, a heroic figure overcoming adversity, or a tragic victim of malicious and envious critics. Whatever the persona chosen, Erasmus was firmly in control of the image projected.

In the *Compendium* Erasmus is vague about the year of his birth. Modern historians and evidence from his own writings suggest the year 1466/7.[7] His parents, Margaret and Gerard, were never married. Erasmus claims that his father's family prevented the marriage by means of a devious plot. The family had destined Gerard for the Church.

> All agreed that out of so large a family one should be consecrated to God. You know how old men feel. And his brothers [there were nine!] wished to have no reduction in their own patrimony, but someone with whom they could always be sure of a dinner. Gerard, finding himself entirely debarred by general consent from matrimony did what men in despair often do: he ran away.[8]

Margaret, who was expecting his child, was left behind. When Gerard's parents discovered their son's whereabouts, they wrote and informed him that the young woman had died. Gerard, who had been making a living as a copyist in Rome, sought consolation in religion and became a priest. On returning home, he discovered that the story of Margaret's death had been concocted by his parents. He provided for his son's education, but both he and Margaret fell victim to a plague epidemic, leaving Erasmus an orphan at the age of 13.

Several details in this story have been manipulated to improve the overall picture. Erasmus tells us nothing, for example, about a brother, Pieter, three years his senior. There are several explanations for this omission. The existence of an older brother puts a different construction on his parents' relationship. It can no longer be seen as a brief passionate affair, but appears as deliberate and prolonged disregard for the laws of the Church. Alternatively, Erasmus may have omitted any mention of Pieter out of consideration for his brother. Both boys were after all subject to the stigma and legal barriers of illegitimacy. Persons born out of wedlock were required to obtain dispensations to hold an ecclesiastical benefice, to obtain a university degree, or to make a will. Erasmus had obtained the necessary papers through the good services of friends in high places, but his brother was still subject to the penalties associated with illegitimacy. It is also possible that he did not wish to mention his brother's name because Pieter's conduct was an embarrassment to him. In another autobiographical account meant for the eyes of the cardinal promoting Erasmus's cause in Rome, he tells us that Pieter was never anything but an 'evil genius' to him. He had 'an eye to the main chance, was not above stealing money, a sturdy drinker and as a wencher far from idle; in short so unlike his younger brother that you might think he was a changeling.'[9]

Erasmus's tale of his parents' frustrated wedding plans also raises questions. The papal dispensation granted him in 1516 indicates that there was more than parental disapproval behind Gerard's failure to marry the mother of his children.[10] The document calls Erasmus 'the offspring of an unlawful and (as he fears) incestuous and condemned union'.[11] The terminology suggests that Erasmus's parents were related, perhaps by marriage, in a degree that violated the canonical rules, thus making their union technically 'incestuous'. One need only think of Henry VIII and his 'great matter' to understand the troublesome nature of the ecclesiastical laws governing consanguinity.

In the *Compendium* Erasmus goes on to relate the further tribulations of his youth. He had been left in the hands of three guardians, who mismanaged the funds entrusted to them by Gerard. When the boy expressed a desire to go to university, the guardians demurred. 'They were afraid of a university, for they had already decided to bring up the boy for the life of a religious.'[12] Has there ever been a young man who did not feel misunderstood by his parents, or in this case, the men who stood *in loco parentis*? Erasmus was in love with the Muses. 'A kind of secret natural force had swept me into liberal studies', he wrote.[13] His guardians took a more practical view of the future and Erasmus's chances of making a living. An academic career was a pipedream. The lucrative professions – law, medicine, theology – required many years of study and were costly.

And even more costly in Erasmus's case, since he would have to obtain a dispensation to graduate. It might take a teenage boy three years to obtain a BA, another two years to obtain an MA, and after that a minimum of six years to graduate from the higher faculties. The majority of students left without a degree, eking out a living as tutors or scribes or proofreaders, moving from place to place in search of a generous patron to whom they could attach themselves as secretaries. More often than not, they lived from hand to mouth, too poor to register on taxation records. In his youthful optimism, Erasmus was convinced that he would succeed at university. '[I] shall not want friends, and many people who possess absolutely nothing maintain themselves by their own efforts. In the end, God will be with us if our purpose is honourable.'[14] No doubt, Erasmus's guardians thought it wiser to invest the little money he had in the Church and to find him a place in a monastery. It was an efficient, safe and respectable way of discharging their responsibilities, and would protect their young charge against the vicissitudes of life.[15] The difference of opinion led to a confrontation between Erasmus and one of his guardians, which is dramatized in the *Compendium*.

> When the plan had been explained to him] the youth answered sensibly, that he did not yet know what the world was, or what a monastery was, or what he was himself; and so it seemed, he said, a better plan that he should still spend some years attending lectures, until he might know his own mind better. When he saw the young man persist in this, [the guardian] suddenly lost his temper. 'I see,' he said, 'I have wasted my labour in securing you a place [at a monastery] with so much entreaty. You are a worthless fellow, and have a spirit of perversity in you. I resign my office as guardian. You can fend for yourself.' The youth replied that he accepted his resignation, being now of an age when guardians were no longer necessary. When the man saw that threats got him nowhere, he suborned his brother, who was also one of the trustees, and a man of business, and set to work with blandishments.[16]

The guardian also enlisted the help of one Cornelis of Woerden, a childhood friend of Erasmus, who had entered the house of the Augustin-ian Canons at Steyn. The young man was able to persuade him to join that religious community, painting a picture that was no more realistic than Erasmus's idea of life among the Muses. He spoke of a 'very saintly way of life, with plenty of books, leisure, tranquillity and a society like that of angels'.[17] What Erasmus found, after taking his vows in 1488, was a community of monks who shared in the common flaws of humanity and a way of life that was much too regulated for his taste.

In 1514, after he had obtained permission to live outside the monastery, he justified his departure by describing the conditions at Steyn. He reiterated that the monastic life had been forced on him and that he was unsuited for it both physically and mentally. He expressed satisfaction that he was now living 'among men of sobriety and among literary studies' and pointedly noted that his present society had 'the true flavour of Christianity'.[18] By contrast,

> whenever I thought about rejoining the community [at Steyn], I envisaged the envy of many, the contempt of all, the conversations so cold and inept, with no savour of Christ, the banquets so profane in their spirit, in short the whole tenor of life such that, if the ceremonies were removed, I cannot see what would be left that was desirable.[19]

Here as in other apologetic writings, he mentioned his constitutional weakness, 'now increased by age, sickness, and toil'.[20] Even as a child he had had a 'delicate physique, though adequate for the activities of the mind'.[21]

Erasmus was about 19 years old when he entered Steyn. In the *Compendium*, he supplies no dates and leaves readers with the impression that he was pressured into making his profession at a tender age. He writes that he was kept from changing his course 'partly by natural shyness, partly by threats and partly by necessity'.[22] No doubt, his options at that time were limited. Similar explanations for his unhappiness at Steyn appear some 20 years later in his appeal to Pope Leo X for dispensation from apostasy and permission to continue living outside the monastery as a secular priest. His request was granted, as the papal letter states, because he had made his profession under duress rather than 'of his own free will'.[23]

When Erasmus first entered the monastery, he attempted to continue his humanistic studies, but his superiors frowned on the pursuit of secular learning, and he was forced to conceal his interests. 'He used secretly to go through a whole comedy of Terence [with Cornelis of Woerden] sometimes in a single night, so that within a few months they went right through the principal authors in these furtive and nocturnal sessions, to the great peril of his delicate health.'[24] The correspondence Erasmus carried on in those years, either as a form of writing exercise or because the monastic routine did not allow him to converse freely with others, shows him opening his heart to his companions and proselytizing on behalf of humanistic studies. A certain youthful fervour and warmth of expression, especially in his letters to Servatius Rogerus, later prior of Steyn, has prompted speculation about a homosexual relationship, but in that case Erasmus would hardly have published the correspondence himself. In fact he candidly spoke of his 'strong boyish affection' for Cornelis of Woerden, and noted that it was 'not uncommon at this age to conceive passionate attachments for some of your companions', a fact also acknowledged in modern psychology.[25] The phrases he employed in his affectionate letters may raise eyebrows among modern readers, but reflect the rhetorical taste of the age. Erasmus's own manual of style, which was used widely in schools, gives us a sense for the topos of friendship. The handbook provides collections of commonplaces arranged by subject matter. Among the possible variants for the sentiment 'I shall always remember you' we find a great deal of what we would now regard as gushing emotion:

> While I enjoy the light of life, you shall be fixed in my thoughts.
> Life shall desert me not a moment later than the remembrance of one so dear.
> Save only death, no mischance shall cast you forth from my heart.
> Could I ever while alive forget so delightful a companion?
> You are too dear to my heart ever to pass into forgetfulness, at least while I have life.
> While any spark of vital heat shall pulse within this breast my remembrance of you shall never fade away.
> As long as any vein shall pulse with vital heat, to remember you shall ever prove delightful.

These flowerets are followed by several hundred more.[26] A familiarity with humanistic usage helps to put the relationship between Erasmus and his friends in perspective. Homoerotic feelings may have played a role, but there is no evidence of sexual misconduct on Erasmus's part at that or any other time in his life. He was accused by his enemies of tippling, flattery, undue ambition, hypocrisy and caustic humour, but never of what was in his time condemned as unnatural sexual relations. On the contrary, it was felt that he was too partial to heterosexual practices and praised marriage too liberally. His declamation *In Praise of Marriage* made at least one cleric wonder about the source of his knowledge and opine that he was 'in the category of adulterers or rapists or fornicators'.[27] The vice-chancellor of the University of Louvain was so incensed by the content of the declamation, which gave preference to marriage over celibacy, that he digressed from his prepared speech on the occasion of a graduation ceremony to lash out against the author. He was especially offended by Erasmus's notion that sexual desire was natural, need not be baulked and should be used for its God-given purpose, namely procreation within marriage.[28] In his defence, Erasmus pointed out that he had also written compositions in praise of celibacy and monastic vows. A short treatise on this subject, entitled *On Disdaining the World*, has the appearance of a rhetorical exercise, because it argues on both sides of the question. In the first eleven chapters, Erasmus praised monastic life. In the last chapter he introduced counter-arguments.[29] A closer look at the genesis of the work suggests that Erasmus wrote the first eleven chapters as a young canon for his own benefit or consolation, attempting in effect to make an irreversible step more palatable. The last chapter, which was added at a later time, contains warnings equally pertinent to his own experience: that the monastic life was not for everyone, that the reality was far from the proclaimed monastic ideal, that many young people were forced or tricked into taking the vows before they understood their own predilections and weaknesses.

In 1493 Erasmus was rescued from the cloistered life. Hendrik of Bergen, bishop of Cambrai, was the *deus ex machina*[30] who effected his release. The bishop had hopes of a cardinalate and needed a secretary who had the rhetorical skills to carry on his correspondence with the powers that be. When the bishop's efforts failed and he no longer had any need for Erasmus's services he sent him to Paris to study, that is to say, to receive instruction in theology at the Collège de Montaigu, a college for poor students. In the *Compendium* Erasmus contented himself with a brief remark that he owed his weak constitution to the 'rotten eggs' and 'infected lodgings' at the college. In one of his *Colloquies*, published in 1526, however, he added dramatic flourishes to the picture:

That college was then ruled by Jan Standonck, a man whose intentions were beyond reproach but whom you would have found entirely lacking in judgement. Because he remembered his own youth, which had been spent in bitter poverty, he took special account of impoverished students. For that he deserves much credit. And had he relieved the poverty of young men enough to provide a decent support for honest studies, while making sure that they did not have too soft a life, he would have merited praise. But this he tried to do by means of bedding so hard, diet so harsh and scanty, by sleepless nights and labours so burdensome, that within a year his initiative had caused the deaths of many very capable, gifted, promising youths and brought others (some of whom I myself knew) to blindness, nervous breakdowns, or leprosy. Not a single student in fact was out of danger . . . To restrain licentious youth by counsels of moderation is a paternal office. But in the cold of midwinter those who ask for food are given a bit of bread; they are told to drink from a well that is pestilential or is dangerous, even if it has only the chill of the early morning. I know many who even today can't shake off the illness contracted there. On the ground floor were cubicles with rotten plaster, near stinking latrines. No one ever lived in these without either dying or getting a terrible disease. I omit for the present the astonishingly savage floggings, even of the innocent. Thus, they declare, is 'wildness' tamed – 'wildness' being their name for unusual talent, which they zealously destroy, to render men more fit for monasteries . . . I've judged it worthwhile to warn against human cruelty corrupting inexperienced and tender youth under the guise of religion. How much politeness or true religion is learned there nowadays I don't, at the moment, inquire. But if I saw that everyone who put on a cowl put off his sinfulness, I'd urge everybody to don a cowl.[31]

Erasmus's stay in Paris, which remained his place of residence on and off for almost five years (1495–99), has often been misrepresented. He was not enrolled at the university, and he did not take a degree.[32] Rather, he attended lectures in theology given at the college. In his autobiographical sketch he makes much of the bishop's failure to provide financial support, but comments only briefly on his own motivation: 'Theology repelled him, for he felt himself not disposed to undermine all its foundations with the prospect of being branded as a heretic.'[33] This terse comment may have spoken volumes to his contemporaries but needs contextualizing for the modern reader. The theology taught at Paris was scholastic theology, which focused on Aristotelian logic and the method of dialectical disputation. The study of the Bible, based on the Latin Vulgate, was mediated through medieval commentaries. As a budding humanist, Erasmus adhered to the principle *Ad fontes*, that is, he advocated the study of the biblical text in the original languages and preferred the commentaries of the Early Church Fathers to the expositions of medieval exegetes. Like all humanists, he despised the pedestrian Latin of medieval writers and called for a return to the classical idiom. A self-caricature from the year 1499 cleverly incorporated the humanistic critique of scholastic theology.

In it Erasmus described himself as attending lectures with 'furrowed brow, uncomprehending look and worried expression'. Scholastic theology was completely alien to him.

> The secrets of this branch of learning cannot be grasped by a person who has anything at all to do with the Muses or the Graces; for this, you must unlearn any literary lore you have put your hands on, and vomit up any draught you have drunk from Helicon. So I am trying with might and main to say nothing in good Latin, or elegantly, or wittily; and I seem to be making progress; so there is some hope that, eventually, they will acknowledge me [as a theologian].[34]

Although distaste for scholastic theology no doubt played an important role in Erasmus's failure to persevere in his studies, he put the blame on material circumstances: 'There, with no patron to support him, it was a question of survival rather than study.'[35] Erasmus accordingly left the Collège de Montaigu and struck out independently as a tutor of wealthy young men. A tutor's position was not easy, given his social disadvantage. He had to keep a fine balance between gaining the goodwill of his charges and keeping discipline, between fraternizing and maintaining his authority: in other words, between pleasing the young man and pleasing his parent. From his pedagogical tracts, we may judge that Erasmus was sensitive to the needs of the learner. Composing his own textbooks, such as *Formulae of Colloquies* or *On Writing Letters*, he tried to combine instruction with entertainment. In a letter intended as a model of epistolary style for his pupil Heinrich Northoff, he describes the ideal learning environment, or rather, he depicts himself and his students as the ideal academic community:

> [On a fine summer day, we went for a stroll] to the very place, as Erasmus proceeded to tell us, he had sometimes walked with you [Heinrich's brother] when you wandered together, drunk on honey-sweet talk and dodging between the vineyards, while he employed those eloquently persuasive arguments of his to summon you away from vulgar cares to a wholehearted love of letters. Do you recognize the spot, Christian? It was there that Erasmus entertained us with a literary recital that was far more elegant even than the supper: he rehearsed so much ancient lore, in so charming a manner, that, to speak for myself, he transported me to the seventh heaven.[36]

In another letter that may have been intended as a model invective, Erasmus described a case in which he gained the affection of his pupil, the young Englishman Thomas Grey, but greatly displeased his guardian and was dismissed as a result. The old man, Erasmus says, was envious of his charge's success:

> Alas for the envious malice of old men, the most monstrous vice one could mention or imagine. Having themselves passed their lives, as you would expect, in debauchery, they are wretchedly envious of you, who are young and better endowed and at a better time of life, because you betook yourself earlier to the humanities. They are envious because the warm blood leaps in your breast, whereas they themselves have only hearts of lead. And so they endeavour to delay you as you run ahead, instead of urging you on as they should, while they themselves, unfit to follow, try to take the lead.[37]

Erasmus takes a literary revenge on the man by describing him as monstrously ugly: 'Beneath a forest of shaggy eyebrows lurk shifty eyes that always glower at you . . . His forehead is granite. There is no vestige of a modest blush, even in the cheeks. His nostrils are choked with thickets of bristly hair; his breath snuffles through a polyp. His jowls sag; his lips are pale', and so forth in the same tenor.[38] He continued to teach Thomas by correspondence, once again depicting the ideal of an intellectual friendship between teacher and student as 'an honourable love'. Physical separation cannot destroy their love; a lasting bond has been created by their common interest in learning.[39]

Another of Erasmus's students, William Blount, Lord Mountjoy, formed an enduring friendship with him and became an important patron. The young man was about 19 years old in 1498, when he was tutored by Erasmus in Paris. He invited his teacher to accompany him on his return journey to England the following year. The account Erasmus gives of that visit and a second sojourn in England during 1505/6 is surprisingly concise and devoid of expressions of gratitude for the generosity of the English patrons, to whose notice he came on those occasions. Rather, his account focuses on a single incident that was ruinous for him at the time but which pales in importance by comparison with the lasting benefits he derived from his new associations. Thus he says, rather ungenerously, that he 'visited England to oblige Mountjoy' and omits the fact that the latter supported him for the remainder of his life with an annual pension.[40] Nor does he mention Thomas More, although he had stayed at his house, collaborated with him on translations from the Greek, and formed a lifelong friendship. The reader is never allowed to forget that Erasmus is the hero of the story: 'He won the good opinion of all men of standing in England, particularly because although robbed on the coast at Dover, he not only sought no revenge but published a short work not long after in praise of the king of England and the whole country.'[41] He describes this episode in more detail elsewhere. He had been assured that currency could be exported, but when he left England, customs confiscated most of his money. 'Many people expected me to avenge this misfortune with my pen, as men of letters normally do, but I was not so prejudiced as to blame my private mishap on a whole country.'[42] On the contrary, he dedicated his collection of adages to Mountjoy and added a poem in praise of Britain. After this self-congratulatory account, Erasmus mentions that he 'secured the friendship of [William Warham], the Archbishop of Canterbury', once again omitting any reference to his generous patronage.[43] 'When [certain] offers did not materialize, he set off for Italy, which he had always had a great desire to visit.'[44] There, he tells us, he

would not have failed to secure a lucrative position had he not been summoned back to England on the death of Henry VII and accession of Henry VIII by letters from friends, full of generous promises. In England he had decided to spend the rest of his life; but as these promises were no more kept now than before, he retreated to Brabant, having been invited to the court of the present Emperor Charles, whose councillor he became through the efforts of the Lord Chancellor, Jean Le Sauvage.[45]

This concise passage describing the decade 1506–16 contains a number of significant omissions. Only half a dozen letters survive from the period during which he travelled in Italy. From them and from other sources we know that Erasmus obtained a doctorate of theology from the University of Turin and spent almost a year in the house of the famous Venetian printer Aldo Manuzio, who reprinted his *Adages* and employed him as editor and proofreader. Erasmus rarely mentions his doctorate, which was obtained *per saltum*, that is, without fulfilling the normal residence requirements and passing the usual examinations. His discretion is understandable when one considers his relentless lampooning of academic theologians. Nor was the manner in which he obtained the degree likely to impress readers. Indeed, even during his lifetime, graduates of the prestigious university of Paris refused to acknowledge him as a fellow-theologian and questioned the value of his degree.[46] Another glaring omission in the *Compendium* concerns the two ecclesiastical benefices bestowed on Erasmus through the generosity of William Warham and Jean Le Sauvage.[47] His reticence on this point in the auto-biographical sketch betrays his concern that the acquisition of the two livings might cast him in an unfavourable light. After all, pluralism, non-residence and the practice of converting Church offices to pensions were regarded as abuses and became prominent targets of reformation theologians.

Two factors mitigate the seriousness of Erasmus's omissions. The sketch is clearly only a collection of notes to be fleshed out by Goclenius; and several of his patrons, mentioned only in passing in the *Compendium*, are given generous praise elsewhere. Erasmus specifically points Goclenius to the *Catalogue of Works*, recommending it as a supplementary source of information. There, for example, Thomas More is praised as 'the most upright, fair-minded, friendly, intelligent man on whom the sun has shone for many generations'.[48] Yet, the *Catalogue* contains the same apologetic tendencies and self-important posturing as the *Compendium*, and we must assume that the autobiographical sketch was meant to focus Goclenius's attention on what was said and subtly steer him away from what remained unsaid.

The sketch concludes with a few words about Erasmus's character, another clear attempt to guide Goclenius. Erasmus singles out three qualities: love of the truth, disdain for money and distaste for polemics. Few of his contemporaries would have accepted his claim to those virtues without qualification. Several of his correspondents accused him of the corresponding vices. Erasmus's relativism ('The truth does not always have to be told, and it matters a great deal how it is told') was notorious.[49] He was repeatedly accused of truckling to patrons and opposing Luther to please popes and princes who offered generous rewards. Polemics filled one in nine volumes of the *Opera omnia* published by Froben in 1540. As one of his Italian opponents noted: 'You get angry and rush into polemics if anyone as much as touches you.'[50] Most significantly, Beatus Rhenanus, who became Erasmus's biographer after Goclenius' death in 1539, passed over his supposed love of the truth and spirit of compromise. Among the virtues he singled out were liberality, loyalty to friends and wit. These were the qualities that made him '*erasmios*, that is, lovable.'[51]

The catalogue of works, which Erasmus mentions in his letter to Goclenius as another biographical source, was published in 1523. It was written at the request of Johann Botzheim, a collector of Erasmian works, who found the many reprints and revisions confusing. In response Erasmus prepared an annotated list of his works. The Froben press, then Erasmus's principal publisher, apparently found the list a useful advertising tool. It issued updated versions of the catalogue in 1524 and 1537, and in 1540 placed a third revised edition among the introductory pieces of Erasmus's *Opera omnia.*

In the catalogue, Erasmus arranges his works under nine headings: works furthering language arts; adages, which were 'not alien to the first category'; correspondence; works furthering moral education (Erasmus notes that some works listed in the first category might also be included here); works promoting piety; the annotated edition of the New Testament; the paraphrases on the New Testament; the apologiae; and a selection of editions and translations of patristic works.[52] The list of works is preceded by a descriptive part which modern readers at any rate will find lacking in structure and encumbered with apologetic asides and lengthy anecdotes. However, this informal approach is typical of humanistic discourse. It mimics conversation and shies away from the tight structure preferred by the humanists' arch-enemies: the scholastics. Erasmus goes to considerable lengths to give the catalogue the appearance of a personal letter. He begins with compliments for Botzheim, addresses him throughout the rambling narrative, and ends with a discussion of a new remedy for kidney stones and greetings to mutual friends. Although this casual presentation of his life's work is not without charm, it assumes that the reader, like the addressee of the 'letter', has some familiarity with Erasmus's literary output. In my summary here, I will adopt a more functional arrangement based on the professional role adopted by Erasmus in a given group of works. He variously wrote as a philologist, educator, moralist, social commentator, biblical humanist and theologian. These functions broadly match the chronology of his life, mirroring his professional development and indicating the focus of his interests during successive phases.

Erasmus began as a humanist in the fifteenth-century sense of the word: a philologist and teacher of language arts. One of his earliest works, therefore, the unfinished dialogue *Antibarbari*, composed in the 1480s, is a defence of humanistic studies. The bulk of his output in the 1490s was study aids. These included manuals on letter-writing and style, collections of proverbs, similes and historical anecdotes for the embellishment of compositions, dialogues ('colloquies') to teach boys good Latin, a Greek grammar, translations of classical Greek texts and model declamations. Education, which provided the focus of his earliest writings, remained an

Erasmian preoccupation throughout his life. After all, he believed that 'man was not born but made human through education' and that education contributed substantially to his life.[53] While Erasmus's earliest writings provided practical aids, he soon followed up with a theory of education and curriculum proposals, among them, *Methodus verae theologiae*, *Ratio studiorum* and *De pueris instituendis*. And he returned to the theme of education in his last work, *Ecclesiastes*, which offered instruction to preachers.

Humanistic pedagogy always had a moral dimension, and Erasmus's philosophy of education is no exception. Many of his teaching materials are moralizing in content, but he began focusing specifically on moral teaching in the early 1500s, composing a number of hortatory and devotional works. In the catalogue, he lists among the books 'that contribute to moral education' his famous satire, *Moria* (1509), the *Panegyricus* (1504) which describes the ideal ruler under the guise of conventional praise for Philip the Fair, the *Institutio principis christiani* (1516), treating of the same subject and addressed to Philip's son Charles, and the *Querela pacis* (1517), a eulogy of peace. The last three works contain elements of political theory, which in Erasmus's eyes was inseparable from Christian ethics. The finest quality of the ruler was 'being pre-eminent in holiness' and to 'govern his realm according to the example of God'.[54] It is significant that Erasmus's catalogue contains books in the categories of 'promoting morals' and 'promoting piety', but lacks a category for theological writings. This indicates that works such as his psalm commentaries were homiletic as much as exegetical. They contained excurses on the war against the Turks and on the reunification of the Church, which combined political with moral counsel and were 'exegetical' only in so far as they took their departure from a line in the psalms. Similarly, Erasmus's treatise on dietary restrictions (*De esu carnium*, 1522), on confession (*Exomologesis*, 1525) and on free will (*De libero arbitrio*, 1524) had more than doctrinal significance. They were, respectively, pleas for the deregulation of religion, criticism of abusive practices and a display of the method Erasmus regarded as most appropriate in dealing with doctrinal questions. On the whole, he was inclined to focus on piety rather than orthodoxy and to adopt the role of a spiritual counsellor rather than a political adviser or a theologian. The attacks of theologians on his work, however, forced him to go against his inclinations. To refute their charge of incompetence, he was obliged to enter the arena on their terms and play the theologian as best he could.

Erasmus began to take a serious interest in biblical studies under the influence of John Colet, whose acquaintance he had made on his first visit to England in 1499. He may be projecting backward when he tells us that his translations of classical Greek texts were nothing but stepping-stones to his study of the biblical text. He was at any rate well qualified for the task when he undertook a critical edition of the New Testament. The first edition, which appeared in 1516, offered a Greek text (the *editio princeps*) faced by a revised Vulgate translation, both based on a fresh collation of manuscripts. The annotations accompanying the text were at first concerned mainly with philological points, but as Erasmus came under attack from theologians, their substance changed. In an effort to defend himself and shore up his text and interpretation, he added to later editions of his New Testament a large number of quotations from patristic writings and numerous references, mostly critical, to medieval exegetes. The quotations from patristic texts were the fruit of his work on Jerome, Augustine, Origen, Chrysostom and many other prominent Church Fathers, whose writings he edited and translated in the 1520s and 1530s. Paraphrases of the gospels and epistles, written in a homiletic style, and commentaries on a number of psalms rounded off his contribution to biblical studies.

Although Erasmus continued to produce original works during the last decade of his life, notably the *Ciceronianus* and the *Ecclesiastes*, both of which examine the style appropriate to Christian speakers, his literary output was overshadowed by polemics. Among Catholic opponents, the theologians of Louvain and Paris tended to be his most persistent critics, as evidenced in his polemics against Maarten van Dorp, Briard of Ath, Edward Lee and Jacques Masson (all at Louvain), and against Noël Béda, Josse Clichtove and Pierre Cousturier (Paris doctors). The Louvain controversies were silenced by papal and imperial decrees imposing a moratorium on the warring parties. Both Erasmus and Masson therefore left polemical tracts unpublished. In Paris, however, Béda was successful in mobilizing the faculty and orchestrating an official censure of Erasmus's works. A similar initiative in Spain was quashed since the Erasmians at the imperial court wielded considerable power. Erasmus, however, answered both the official censures of Paris and the unpublished complaints of the Spanish theologians and carried on a lengthy feud with Diego López Zúñiga, a theologian at Alcala, who had attacked his edition of the New Testament. In Rome, successive popes discouraged open criticism of Erasmus to avoid driving him into the enemy camp. Thus López Zúñiga, who had moved to Rome, saw his efforts to publish attacks on Erasmus repeatedly frustrated. By contrast, Alberto Pio, one of

Erasmus's most vocal opponents at the papal court, fled to Paris after the sack of Rome (1527) and found a receptive audience in Béda's circle.

Several of the Catholic polemicists are mentioned by Erasmus in his catalogue and disparaged with considerable warmth. Masson's attack, Erasmus said, reflected 'his powers of malignant invention'; López Zúñiga was 'boastful, shameless, stupid, a great admirer of his own perfections' and his book was 'full of extraordinary delusions'. Dismissing his critics as malicious, Erasmus fails to address the serious issues underlying the controversies: questions concerning teaching authority and the competency of men, such as himself, who had no professional theological training; questions concerning divine inspiration, whether it covered the original biblical author as well as the translator and protected him from errors in fact as well as errors in style. These questions require a close reading of his polemics, and I shall return to them in Chapter 5.

Erasmus's initial effort to stay on the sidelines of the Reformation debate, and his eventual rejection of the reformers' programme, exposed him to attacks from that quarter as well. These too are reflected in the catalogue. 'Erasmus laid the egg, and Luther hatched it' was a popular tag in the 1520s. Erasmus denied that he had prepared the way for Luther and complained that books, such as the *Enchiridium* (1504), which he had written before calls for reform turned into a schismatic movement, were reinterpreted in light of later developments and given a heterodox twist. In the catalogue he complained, moreover, that some of the dialogues added to later editions of his *Colloquies* and containing criticism of Church abuses were given a more sinister interpretation than they deserved. 'As long as there was nothing in that book but the merest trifles, it found surprising favour on all sides. When it began to be useful in many ways, it could not escape the poison-fangs of slander. A certain divine in Louvain, who is physically purblind and mentally even more so, detected in it four passages that were heretical.'[55] A number of theologians were now connecting humanism with the Reformation, linking the humanistic call to the sources with Luther's principle of *sola scriptura*. Erasmus labelled this confusion of issues a conspiracy and claimed that it was a strategy employed by scholastic theologians to ruin both movements at one strike.

Until Luther's official condemnation in 1521, Erasmus had indeed been supportive of the reformer, although he was critical of his aggressive style. After 1521, when it became clear that the movement was heading towards schism, Erasmus drew back. Many in the reform party who had hoped that Erasmus would exert his influence on their behalf interpreted this change as cowardice and hypocrisy. In the catalogue Erasmus acknowledged that he was not prepared to become a martyr to the Reformation movement, but stressed that disapproval rather than lack of courage was holding him back. 'They [the reformers] have nothing they can bring against me except that I am reluctant to risk my own neck by professing beliefs which I do not hold, or regard as doubtful, or reject, and which would do no good if I did profess them.' He emphasized that he had spoken out on issues that he shared with the reformers: putting too much trust in ceremonies, giving more weight to human than to scriptural precepts, superstitious practices, the corruption of academic theology.

> This, and very much else, which I have taught according to the measure of grace accorded me, I have taught steadfastly, but never standing in the way of any man who had something better to teach. And they say Erasmus has taught nothing but rhetoric! I wish they would persuade . . . those foolish babblers who steadfastly maintain that all Luther's teaching has been drawn from what I have written.

He protested against the radicalism of the reformers, their 'mad-dog scurrility [which] can produce nothing but sedition and bloodshed', contrasting it with his own moderation and love of peace: 'My misdeeds amount to this: I am all for moderation, and the reason why I have a bad name with both sides is that I exhort both parties to adopt a more peaceable policy.'[56]

While he put his finger on an important factor causing tensions between him and the reformers, Erasmus did not elaborate on a more important point: the underlying epistemological differences. His scepticism obliged him to rely on consensus as a decision-making tool. His pacifism, therefore, was not merely a moral stand or a personal inclination but had epistemological significance as well. A philosophical discussion was, however, inappropriate in a catalogue whose principal function was advertising the author's (and publisher's) wares. The journalistic style and occasionally strident tone served this purpose well. For the philosophical and theological context of Erasmus's polemics and the principles guiding his argumentation we must look to his controversies, notably his polemic with Luther over the question of free will, which will concern us in Chapter 6.

Although the catalogue does not provide a thoroughgoing analysis of Erasmus's work, it does contribute to a better understanding of the authorial voice. In the introductory section, Erasmus speaks at some length about the writer's standards and his choice of topics. A man's books, he says, reflect the cultural context of his time. 'The generation and the country in which you write make a great difference.' In his case, 'time and place were unpropitious', for humanism had barely penetrated Northern Europe when he was a young man. He was, moreover, too obliging, allowing friends and publishers to dictate the subject of his research or at any rate divert him to a particular subject. Ideally, an author 'should choose a subject to which he is by nature suited, in which his powers chiefly lie; all themes do not suit everyone'. Erasmus discovered this too late. He 'either stumbled on a subject inadvisedly or chose one to comply with [his] friends' feelings rather than [his] own judgement'. His inclination was to publish hurriedly. 'Once I have embarked on a subject,' he wrote, 'I generally run through to the finish without a break, and I have never been able to stomach the tedium of revision.' This meant that mistakes went uncorrected and necessitated a second edition. In his biographical sketch, Erasmus put a different construction on the numerous editions of his works: he was a perfectionist. 'Having a touch of pedantry, he never wrote anything with which he was satisfied.'[57] The contradiction between the two explanations shows once again that his autobiographical writings are a constructive exercise. They are less a reflection of a life lived than a projection of a life suitable for publication.

The catalogue also includes remarks on Erasmus's financial situation. He speaks coyly of the income he derived from his literary activities and disparages the notion that dedications made him 'as rich as Midas'. Commenting on the generosity of friends and patrons, he assures his readers first of all that it was unsolicited and that 'it comes far more easily to me to express refusal than acceptance'. He emphasizes, moreover, that he took greater pleasure in the kindness and recognition implied by monetary gifts than in the gifts themselves. Nevertheless, he singled out by name several dedicatees who did not reward him financially. From Leo X, for example, he 'neither expected nor received a single ducat'. Similarly, Cardinal Grimani, 'did not send me a farthing, nor did I expect it'. He did not wish to embarrass these men or criticize their lack of generosity in an backhanded way, but wanted to document that he had not been 'bribed' by Catholic prelates to remain in the Catholic fold – as had been suggested by his enemies. A long list follows which supplies readers with detailed accounts of goods, money or church offices tendered to him, some accepted, others declined. He concludes with the noble sentiment that he 'reckons any profit that accrues to humane studies as though it were money in my own purse'.[58] He fixes his annual pensions at 400 gold florins, adding that

> this fortune is unequal, I confess, to the expenses demanded by my age and state of health, by the assistance which my work must have in the way of servants and transcribers, by my keeping a horse, by my constant journeys, and by a spirit (to give it no other name) that will not tolerate meanness and squalor, that abhors bills unpaid, services unrequited, and friends neglected in their distress.[59]

The financial details Erasmus provides, especially the statement that his income was barely enough to maintain the high standard of living to which he had become accustomed, cannot have satisfied those who were jealous of his success. It confirmed, rather than dispelled, the notion that he was well off. Erasmus misjudged the feelings of his readers when he suggested that his account would satisfy them, and 'their criticism should now cease', or when he hoped to appease his critics by scoffing at the need 'to satisfy everyone, even the dregs'.[60] Death at any rate vindicated his claims to philanthropy. His will contained generous provisions to supply destitute young women with dowries and relieve the poverty of deserving young students with bursaries.[61]

2

The fight against the barbarians: Erasmus's educational philosophy

In the last decade of the fifteenth century, when Erasmus wrote a poem *Against the Barbarians who Scorn the Eloquence of the Ancients*,[1] the battle against the 'dark' Middle Ages had already been fought and won by humanists in Italy. Humanism, the cultural and aesthetic movement that dominated the Renaissance, was driven by admiration for the accomplishments of antiquity and a desire to emulate them. The slogan *'Ad fontes'*, calling scholars back to the classical sources, had significant implications for the system of education. A new emphasis on texts and the detailed study of their literary qualities and historically correct interpretation brought about a shift in private education and, eventually, in the curriculum of universities. Literature and language studies began to share the arena previously occupied almost exclusively by logic. This brought the champions of the New Learning, as it was termed, in conflict with the representatives of the traditional medieval curriculum and set the stage for confrontations between humanists and scholastics. The polemic was carried on in Italy as an intellectual debate over the relative merits of rhetoric and philosophy and the pros and cons of Christians studying pagan authors. When the debate was taken up in Northern Europe at the beginning of the sixteenth century, however, it turned into a professional controversy between theologians and teachers of the *studia humaniora*. Fuelled by personal animosities, the conflict became endemic to Northern universities. In the ensuing polemics we find the protagonists of humanism extolling the style and argumentation of classical writings, disparaging the conventions of medieval Latin, and labelling its use as barbarous. They also routinely ridiculed the study of logic, the core subject of the medieval university, as obscurantist quibbling, and demanded equal billing for rhetoric. They denounced the medieval summaries and commentaries on Aristotelian texts as caricatures of his writings, calling for a return to the original text and for the inclusion of other classical authors in the curriculum. In the case of biblical studies, the slogan, *Ad fontes*, meant a return to the Hebrew and Greek texts and to the commentaries of the early Fathers. The involvement of humanists in textual criticism of the Bible incensed scholastic theologians, who questioned their competence and denounced their editorial efforts as impious. At Italian universities humanists were in the ascendant by the second half of the fifteenth century, but in Northern Europe, where theological faculties were powerful, the debate continued unabated.

The advent of humanistic ideas in Northern Europe was also greeted with unease by the regular clergy. In the monastic circles to which Erasmus belonged there were strong misgivings about the humanists' enthusiasm for classical literature. The brethren took to the pulpit to warn against the moral dangers of Christians studying pagan writings. An anecdote related by Erasmus illustrates the prevailing paranoia. As a young man, he tells us, he was commissioned to write a poem on Saint Michael. The patron who had requested it, was appalled when he read the composition submitted by the budding humanist. It was full of classical references. 'One might think it was written in Greek!' was his scandalized reaction. Obviously he regarded 'Greek' as a pejorative epithet.[2]

The fight against the 'barbarians' – the code word widely used in humanistic writings to denote the opponents of the New Learning – was a life-long concern of Erasmus. Two of his earliest extant compositions, the poem *A Sorrowful Dialogue against the Barbarians,* already mentioned, and the *Antibarbari* (Antibarbarians),[3] sound a call to battle. Entering the lists with a tirade against the 'barbarians' was *de rigueur* for young humanists who wished to give proof of their allegiance to the ideals of the New Learning. Erasmus's poem was written *c.* 1498 in collaboration with a friend, the Augustinian canon Cornelis Gerard. The youthful authors lambasted those who spurned eloquence and accused them of envy. The critics, they said, were 'despising what they despaired of achieving'.[4] Erasmus elaborated on this theme in the *Antibarbarians,* purportedly the record of a conversation or debate among friends. The main protagonist of the debate is a schoolmaster, Jacob Batt,[5] who mounts a spirited defence of humanism. He divides the enemies of humanism into three groups: boors who reject classical learning as pagan, claiming that 'to know Greek is heresy, to speak like Cicero is heresy';[6] those who are content with an education that excludes classical learning; and those who have contributed to the decline of classical learning by writing summaries and commentaries, 'shedding darkness on them, not light . . . and turning into bad Latin what was in good Greek'.[7] The three groups represent first the pious hypocrites Erasmus encountered among his fellow canons; secondly the large majority of people who were complacent about learning and satisfied with their accomplishments; and finally the scholastics, whose work had all but replaced the biblical and Aristotelian texts in the university curriculum. Batt's speech is directed primarily against the first group, who reject non-Christian literature out of hand and refuse to consider the merits of the New Learning. Batt points out the absurdity of their arguments. After all, he says, Christian civilization is rooted in the classical tradition and a categorical rejection of pagan learning would deprive the modern world of many advances made in culture and technology. The 'barbarians' protest against reading the classics: 'Virgil is burning in hell, and is a Christian to recite his poems?' Batt counters: 'As if many a Christian were not burning there too! . . . Let us consider the quality of their teaching rather than ask ourselves how well they lived.'[8] He notes that classical rhetoric has not been shunned by St Paul or the Church Fathers. On the contrary, classical learning is highly praised by Jerome and Augustine and is in evidence throughout their writings.

Erasmus himself shows a preoccupation with the question how best to combine the two cultures, to benefit from classical learning while retaining Christian values. In the *Antibarbarians* he suggests that eclecticism is the answer to the dilemma. The student of classical literature should imitate models reflecting Christian virtues and discard those in conflict with them. Reading Plato's dialogues, for example, one might imitate the modesty, learning, and eloquence of Socrates, but not the 'rash garrulity of [the sophist] Gorgias.'[9] The question first raised in the *Antibarbarians*, 'Am I to let myself be called a Ciceronian or a Platonist, when I have once and for all chosen to be called a Christian?'[10] reappears in a late work of Erasmus, entitled *Ciceronianus* (The Ciceronian, 1528). There he discusses the question of *imitatio*, the imitation of classical models. He begins in a bantering tone, lampooning those who idolize Cicero, but continues in a serious vein, attempting to describe the style appropriate to a Christian humanist. The admiration felt by humanists for antiquity must not make them slavish imitators of Cicero, he says. 'All Christian speech should have the savour of Christ, without whom nothing is pleasing or impressive, useful or creditable, stylish or eloquent or learned.'[11] Imitation, as defined by Erasmus, involves an adaptive process. It is more than the incorporation of foreign thought or the transplantation of individual phrases into one's own composition to make it more striking or elegant. Rather, it is the transmission of words and ideas 'to the mind for inward digestion, so that becoming part of your own system, it gives the impression not of something begged from someone else, but of something that springs from your own mental processes, something that exudes the characteristics and force of your own mind and personality'.[12] The key to successful imitation is a sense for *aptum et decorum*, that is, respect for the proper context. The speaker must pay attention to the venue, adapt his speech to the audience and have regard for the timeliness of his remarks. He will not use the same arguments in the pulpit that he would use in a lecture hall or a council meeting. He will not use the same words to address scholars as he would to address the general public. What may have been suitable for the ears of pagans in ancient Rome, may give offence to Christians in papal Rome. Citing a sermon preached at the papal court, in which the homilist referred to Julius II as 'Jupiter Optimus Maximus', Erasmus ridicules and rebukes purists for using the Ciceronian model indiscriminately. He objects to a preacher 'concealing the fact that he is a Christian, or treating Christian subjects in a pagan way'.[13]

When Erasmus advocates a humanistic curriculum, therefore, he advocates reading the pagan sources in a Christian spirit, that is, Christianizing their thought and 'updating' their vocabulary to give expression to new ideas. He classifies the use of post-classical terms in a religious context as technical language. Everyone accepted the fact that there were words 'used in a peculiar sense by rhetoricians, dialecticians and grammarians – words which, except in a technical context, mean something very different or nothing at all'. The Bible, too, had it own *consuetudo*, its own language conventions. It would be peevish of humanists to reject biblical usage, yet tolerate technical terms in rhetoric.[14] Erasmus had not always been so flexible on this point. As a young man he tended to be a purist himself. In his mature writings we find expressions of concern for Christian idiom and a protectiveness about Christian thought that he had earlier disparaged and even labelled hypocritical. He came to admit the danger of students of classical literature 'turning out not Ciceronian but pagan'. He spoke of his own hesitation to change the traditional Vulgate translation in spite of its many grammatical and idiomatic lapses. He might have introduced radical changes, he said, 'had I not wanted to be regarded a Christian rather than a Ciceronian'.[15] This does not mean that Erasmus ended up endorsing the critics lampooned in the *Antibarbarians* or, like them, wanted to see classical studies suppressed. Rather, he wanted to infuse them with a Christian spirit and turn them to a Christian purpose. 'This is the purpose of studying the basic disciplines, of studying philosophy, of studying eloquence', he writes in the *Ciceronian*: 'to know Christ, to celebrate the glory of Christ.'[16]

Erasmus published a number of tracts in which he proffered his philosophy of education. Two of his writings in particular are valuable sources for his thoughts on that subject: *De pueris instituendis* (On the Education of Children, 1529) and *Ecclesiastes* (The Preacher, 1534). In the *Education of Children* Erasmus discusses the obligation of parents to educate their children, the qualities to be looked for in student and tutor respectively, and the teaching practices to be adopted or avoided. *The Preacher*, Erasmus's last original work, combines practical instruction with elements of educational theory, though necessarily within a narrower compass to suit the subject at hand. A third handbook, *Institutio principis Christiani* (The Education of a Christian Prince, 1515), is, in spite of its title, concerned more with political theory than with education and will therefore be discussed in that context. In addition to these works on the theory and practice of education, Erasmus provided detailed curricular models in *De ratione studii* (The Method of Study, 1511) written for young boys, and *Methodus perveniendi ad veram theologiam* (The Systematic Way to True Theology, 1516), written for the benefit of theology students.[17]

In his pedagogical works Erasmus addresses himself almost exclusively to the education of boys, a focus that was conventional and reflected contemporary practice. Statistical evidence suggests that, by the middle of the sixteenth century, almost a third of the male population was literate. The literacy rate for women, however, was significantly lower, standing at 12 per cent. Only about 1 per cent of girls received humanistic training, that is, education in Latin; the rest were taught in the vernacular. The curriculum in girls' schools (parochial or convent schools) was often limited to the Bible, the lives of saints and other spiritual readings.[18]

Renaissance authors frequently raised the question whether women could benefit from education at all. They were inclined to be pessimistic about their abilities or at any rate compared them unfavourably with the intellectual abilities of men. Erasmus himself confessed that he shared these reservations at first, but was convinced by the example of More's daughters that women too could benefit from a liberal education and achieve literary excellence. 'Scarcely any mortal man was not under the conviction that, for the female sex, education had nothing to offer in the way of either virtue or reputation. Nor was I myself in the old days completely free of this opinion; but More has quite put it out of my head.'[19] Erasmus's newfound confidence in the intellectual powers of women was reflected in two colloquies that depicted women challenging the idea of male superiority. In both cases, however, the debate contains a playful element that obscures the message and suggests that Erasmus may have intended to present a paradox rather than a paradigm. In 'The Abbot and the Learned Lady', Margaret (perhaps modelled on More's foster-daughter Margaret Giggs) successfully rebuts a boorish abbot's tirade against learning and in particular against women acquiring an education in the classics. The dialogue ends with Margaret projecting a futuristic scenario: women will preach from the pulpits and lecture at universities. Such a possibility would have struck Erasmus's readers as absurd or para-doxical, and the purpose of the dialogue was more likely to protest the ignorance of the clergy than to eulogize the learning of women. In *The New Mother*, a male visitor raises the question whether a mother should be more pleased with a baby boy than with a baby girl. This leads to a more general discussion of the perceived superiority of men over women. In a mock-scholastic disputation, the young mother cleverly parries the arguments advanced by the visitor in favour of male superiority. Her argu-mentation culminates in the claim that women show more courage in facing childbirth than men in facing the enemy's troops. Again, the purpose is to amuse rather than instruct the reader, and the debate is merely a spirited lead-in to a serious philosophical discussion of the nature of the soul. Erasmus was clearly not in the vanguard of the discussion about women's education or the *querelle feminine*, which reached prominence in the seventeenth century. What little he has to say about the training of girls and young women is kept within the context of a woman's role in the family. The education of a woman, according to Erasmus, is not aimed at self-improvement, or at least not to the degree found in his treatises on the education of boys, but discussed in terms of the benefit to her family and to society at large. He reasons that educated women will be more tractable, 'for nothing is more intractable than ignorance.' They will also be more entertaining: 'One can really enjoy their society. I differ profoundly from those who keep a wife for no purpose except physical satisfaction, for which half-witted females are better fitted.' Education will also make women fit models for their children. Indeed, 'the well-being of society depends' on mothers being trained to provide a suitable setting for the upbringing of their children.[20] One concludes from Erasmus's statements that boys are educated for their own benefit; girls for the benefit of others – a sentiment common in his time. This is not to say that Erasmus was silent on the social benefits of a boy's education. Indeed, the assumption that a good education benefited not only the individual, but also brought distinction to his family and made him an asset to the country, was a commonplace. Erasmus paid homage to that idea in passing, but did not make it a principal consideration as he did in describing the purpose of a woman's education.

Turning to Erasmus's curriculum proposals: we find that they are traditional in the sense that they are extensions of the traditional trivium and quadrivium. At the same time the insistence on training in Greek and Latin was progressive and reflected the ideals of the New Learning first advanced by Italian humanists in the fifteenth century. In both the *Method of Study* and *The Systematic Way to True Theology*, Erasmus places emphasis on the study of Latin and Greek 'because almost everything worth learning is set forth in these two languages'.[21] For theology students, Latin and Greek were important because they were the languages of the Vulgate and of the original text of the New Testament. In addition, Erasmus advocates the study of Hebrew to enable students of theology to read the Old Testament in the original.[22] Although he did not lay down a canon of textbooks for young students, he emphasizes the importance of beginning at once with 'approved authors' (*probati autores)*, for what was the use of wasting one's effort on 'something that you are subsequently compelled to unlearn at even greater effort'?[23] Among 'approved authors', Erasmus includes the rhetorical and philosophical works of Cicero, the poetry of Virgil and Horace, the plays of Terence and the histories of Caesar and Sallust; among the Greek writers, he recommends the prose writers Lucian, Demosthenes and Herodotus and the poets Aristophanes, Homer and Euripides – in that order.[24] Medieval authors (with the exception of the early Fathers) are absent from his humanistic curriculum.

The suggestion that the study of Greek and Latin were basic requirements must have struck some readers as extravagant. A knowledge of Greek was an unusual accomplishment in Northern Europe when Erasmus was a boy. Both Greek texts and Greek teachers were hard to come by, and at most universities lectureships were established only in the second decade of the sixteenth century. Erasmus, who was largely self-taught, recommended translating from Greek into Latin as a 'highly beneficial exercise'.[25] He published his own practice pieces – translations from Euripides, Lucian, Plutarch, Isocrates and others – emphasizing that the authors he had chosen were both interesting and edifying. He praised Plutarch, in particular, for conveying a moral message second only to the Bible. Within a generation, however, Greek became a popular subject, and

Erasmus's curricular proposals were no longer eccentric. He noted without regret – and indeed with some satisfaction – that the demand for his translations fell in the 1530s because the knowledge of Greek had become widespread enough to allow students to read the texts in the original language.

While Erasmus's curriculum proposal for young boys was in the tradition of fifteenth-century Italian humanism and had by the middle of the sixteenth century become widely accepted also in the rest of Europe, his views on the formation of theologians remained controversial throughout his lifetime. Traditionally, professional theologians were trained according to the scholastic method. The emphasis was on Aristotelian logic. Aristotle's writings as well as biblical texts were read in Latin translations. Even more often, students became acquainted with them through the medium of summaries and commentaries written in the Middle Ages. Disputation in the '*sic et non*' style was an integral aspect of scholastic training and occupied much of the student's time. Erasmus disparaged these exercises as training for intellectual sparring and unworthy of a true theologian, who must exert himself for the victory of the truth rather than a personal victory over the opponent in a verbal match. His insistence that a well-rounded theologian must have a knowledge of the biblical languages was a departure from the scholastic tradition, and his advocacy of a philological approach to the interpretation of the text was similarly innovative. Erasmus added the *Methodus*, in which he presented his curriculum proposals, to the prolegomena of his edition of the New Testament. It was a suitable *ouverture* to a work based on insights gained from language studies and demonstrating the mistakes made by translators and interpreters lacking linguistic skills. How can a theologian even follow patristic exegesis, Erasmus asked, 'if he is completely ignorant of the languages on which they are based?' And if the Vulgate translation was sufficient, why did papal decrees instruct clerics 'to seek the original text of the Old Testament in Hebrew writings, and the true reading of the New Testament in the Greek sources?' [26] Indeed, the Bible should be the focus of students of theology. They should have biblical quotations at their fingertips and should read the original texts 'rather than summaries, Bible stories and collections that have been sifted and sifted again six hundred times'. What use was there in learning 'sophistical precepts, Aristotelian commentaries, the conclusions and arguments of [Duns] Scotus, and begrudge the time to Holy Writ, the source from which theology flows in its entirety'?[27] If a student spends all his time on Scotus and similarly 'frigid, specious, thorny and quarrelsome' scholastic authors, he will become like them; whereas if he reads authors that breathe Christ and teach true piety, he will begin to resemble them. Students may object, arguing that scholastic authors prepared them for the required disputations, but Erasmus questions their purpose. 'We are training theologians, not pugilists – theologians, who will express what they teach in their lives rather than their syllogisms.'[28] His emphasis on going back to the sources, in this case the sources of the Christian religion, is a variant on the humanistic call '*Ad fontes*'. In addition to insisting on language studies, Erasmus advised would-be theologians to read the classics to familiarize themselves with the historical context of the Bible. His emphasis on reading the gospels rather than studying Aristotelian philosophy reflects the humanistic preference for ethics over logic and his personal view of the purpose of theological studies. He found fault with setting a purely academic goal. Just as the aim of a liberal education was intellectual as well as moral excellence, so theological studies should equip the graduate with doctrinal knowledge as well as spiritual insight.

Erasmus's proposals dismayed the theological faculty at Louvain, where he resided at the time. The hostile attitude against him was palpable when he became actively involved in the organization of a trilingual college, the legacy of his friend and patron Jerôme Busleyden. Although a truce of sorts was concluded between Erasmus and the theologians, they refused permission to his admirer Alaard of Amsterdam to lecture on the *Ratio* at the Collegium Trilingue.[29] They were, however, unable to suppress the ideas promoted in that work. In the wake of its publication, two young lecturers, Petrus Mosellanus at Leipzig and Philip Melanchthon at Wittenberg, took up the cause and pointed out the importance of language studies for theology students in their inaugural lectures.[30] The Louvain professor Jacques Masson felt obliged to write a rebuttal. In his *De trium linguarum et studii theologici ratione* (On the Three Languages and the Method of Theological Study, 1519), he officially addressed Mosellanus, but quoted from Erasmus's *Ratio*, thus arguing against both men. He emphasized that he appreciated the study of literature, but regarded 'the wicked, corrupt and superstitious stories of Homer and Lucian' dangerous fare for young minds.[31] Nor did he object to the study of the three languages, but linguistic skills were not essential to the theologian. He insisted that the Latin Vulgate and Latin commentaries were all that was needed for a correct exegesis of the Bible. Scholastic commentaries must remain the mainstay of the theology student, he wrote. They provided a bulwark against erroneous interpretations of difficult passages in the Bible, guided the student through the maze of contradictory and antiquated opinions found in patristic writings, and provided the correct answers to questions that had been determined by the Church in the past 300 years. Scholastic doctors were the guardians of orthodoxy; students of theology needed their writings as 'fish needed water'. Masson concluded his work, which was on the whole written in a moderate tone, with a tirade against 'pseudo-theologians' who 'never cease to require in the theologian grammar, languages, and rhetoric . . . and who like a book only if it is pure, correct, and elegant. They defend a man if he cherishes the humanities and reject a book if it is barbarous, that is, not pure Latin.'[32] Masson's rejection of language studies, or at any rate, the notion that they were essential to the theologian, continues to form a theme in controversies pitting Erasmus and other humanists against scholastic theologians. The Paris theologian Noël Béda called Erasmus and Jacques Lefèvre, a French scholar who had applied his philological skills to the Bible, 'theologizing humanists'. When the faculty of theology, on his initiative, censured passages in Erasmus's writings, they likewise issued a general warning against the folly of those 'who think knowing Greek and Hebrew meant being a perfect and consummate theologian'.[33]

Erasmus was undeterred by the pronouncements of the faculty, which wielded considerable power. The need for language studies remains a constant in his writings and is prominent also in his last educational treatise, *Ecclesiastes*, subtitled 'The Art of Preaching'. It is a representative work of Christian humanism. Like Erasmus's two curriculum outlines, it combines classical with Christian precepts and depicts the knowledge of classical languages as an essential skill.[34] Like most Renaissance manuals, *The Preacher* does not aim at originality but offers the reader 'the best of' classical wisdom with a certain updating to reflect contemporary issues and, as is to be expected in a manual on preaching, inject a Christian perspective. Over large stretches of text, Erasmus's instructions read like a summary of Quintilian's or Cicero's rhetorical handbooks. In many instances, however, the classical precepts are deliberately given a Christian content. For example, the classical concept of *ethos* – the good reputation of the speaker which adds credibility to his arguments – reappears, infused with a Christian spirit. The preacher's persuasiveness, Erasmus says, is enhanced by a pure heart; his ministerial authority would be harmed by vice. The Ciceronian idea of the threefold task of the speaker – to instruct, to move, to entertain – is developed and expanded into the mystical idea that the inspired words of a preacher can transform the listeners.[35] The overarching goal of the preacher is to produce piety, to captivate not only the mind but also the soul of the listeners. He must charge his listeners with the moral imperative to act on his arguments and appeal to the congregation's emotions. 'Thus the listener, who is already persuaded and willing himself, will be more easily led to mercy or indignation or penitence.'[36] The classical handbooks note that observing *aptum* and *proprium* assure the speaker's success. They define success as forcing an antagonist to concede victory, obtaining a majority of votes in a political assembly, or a favourable verdict in court. Erasmus's preacher is successful when he glorifies God and benefits his congregation spiritually. His prudence is not only the result of natural talent, practice and experience – the trinity touted by classical pedagogues; it is also a gift of the Holy Spirit.

> Prudence, indeed, is strengthened by education and experience, although natural ability is its principal source. If that natural prudence is present, it acknowledges rather than learns what is taught . . . Yet I do not deny that the prudence found in the sacred orator is a gift of the Holy Spirit. However, that Spirit accommodates its powerful influence to the medium . . . so that the future preacher must be trained.[37]

Thus, humanistic learning and human industry are required to receive the full bounty of the Spirit.

If Erasmus's demand for Greek studies astonished and dismayed theologians, his encouragement to learn Hebrew must have struck them as even more exotic and deliberately provocative in view of the Reuchlin Affair, a cause célèbre which was going through the ecclesiastical courts at the time. The jurist and imperial councillor Johann Reuchlin had been one of the first Christian scholars to promote Hebrew studies north of the Alps. His protest against the confiscation and destruction of Hebrew books instigated by the Jewish convert Johann Pfefferkorn and his Dominican backers, earned him the accusation of being a Judaizer. The charge involved him in a lengthy inquisition which resulted in a verdict of guilty and a fine. The trial did not stigmatize Hebrew studies, as Reuchlin's accusers perhaps had hoped, but gave German humanists a common cause. They published numerous pamphlets and letters in support of Reuchlin and, although they did not succeed in obtaining an acquittal for him, they assured the survival and continued success of Hebrew studies at the universities. Erasmus paid his respects to the Hebrew scholar in a colloquy entitled *The Apotheosis of Reuchlin*, which

reflects Reuchlin's status in the eyes of humanists as a hero and a martyr
to their cause. Erasmus wished to 'keep his memory hallowed, praise his
name, and salute him in this wise: "O sacred spirit, bless languages and
those who study them."'[38]

Although Erasmus consistently advocated Hebrew studies, it is
important to point out certain contradictions in his attitude: an ambivalence which he shared with other humanists. Hebrew was, after all, the
language of the Jews, and even Reuchlin whose commitment to Hebrew
studies cannot be questioned, repeated the old saw that the Jews of his day
were justly suffering persecution to atone for the sins of their fathers who
had crucified Christ.[39] Erasmus was similarly ambivalent. He had begun
to study Hebrew in his thirties, but soon gave it up as too difficult. He
cited his age and a lack of time as factors in abandoning the effort.[40] It
seems, however, that his decision involved a value judgement as well.
This becomes clear from a letter in which he discouraged Wolfgang
Capito, a Basel associate and the author of a Hebrew grammar, from
spending too much time on Hebrew. 'I wish you were more intent on
Greek rather than on those Hebrew studies, although I do not reprehend
them', he wrote.

> I see that that race is full of the most inane fables and succeeds only in
> bringing forth a kind of fog . . . I would rather have Christ tainted by
> [the scholastic] Scotus than by that nonsense . . . I fear that this will be
> an opportunity for the long-suppressed plague to rise up again. I wish
> the Christian Church did not give such weight to the Old Testament! It
> was given for a time only and consists of shadows, yet it is almost
> preferred to Christian writings.

He was concerned that the study of Hebrew might revive Judaism, and
'there is no pestilence more adverse and hostile to the doctrine of Christ
. . . I see how Paul exerted himself to free Christians from Judaism, and I
sense that some people secretely slip back into it'.[41]

The reservations Erasmus expressed to Capito appear to be at odds with
his own practices: his promotion of Hebrew lectures at the trilingual
College at Louvain and his personal engagement in Old Testament
studies. It is difficult to reconcile his warning against 'giving too much
weight to the Old Testament' with the fact that he published no fewer than
eleven psalm commentaries between 1515 and 1536. One might ask
therefore whether anti-Semitism rather than a concern for Christian
values was at the bottom of the misgivings he expressed. The evidence is

mixed. Remarks in letters touching on the Reuchlin affair are clearly anti-Semitic. They are full of angry outbursts against Pfefferkorn. Punning on his name, Erasmus called Pfefferkorn a seed-corn of Satan, a man 'true to his race' and 'infecting the entire population with his Jewish poison'.[42] At the same time, he had praise for the scholarship of the Jewish physician Paolo Ricci and was on good terms with Matthaeus Adrianus, Professor of Hebrew at Louvain.[43] Occasionally he even protested against anti-Semitism: 'If it is Christian to detest the Jews, we are all good Christians, and to spare.'[44] In some of Erasmus's negative remarks, moreover, the designation 'Jew' has no racial overtones and is intended as a metaphor. The 'Jews' he castigates are people who observe the letter rather than the spirit of the law, an attitude commonly associated with the Old Testament. In his preface to the *Paraphrase on John*, for example, Erasmus laments that the world has 'degenerated into a kind of Judaism'. He means that gestures have replaced action. Princes are performing Christian rites without performing their duties as Christian rulers: 'Why is it so important that the prince should say his prayers at regular hours, when he can never find time . . . for the business of the commonwealth?' In a similar vein, he criticizes those who 'put too much trust in ceremonies, displaying more of Judaism than of Christianity'. He wishes 'to arouse a world which allowed too much importance to Jewish ceremonial to a new zeal for the true religion of the Gospel'.[45] Such examples could be multiplied, but an analysis of Erasmus's usage does not entirely resolve the contradictions apparent in his remarks about Jews. It merely shows the need to distinguish between three motives that determined his attitude toward Hebrew studies: his emphasis on piety as an inner quality (which was at odds with the 'Jewish' or Old Testament emphasis on the observance of rites); his phobia of Jews as a race (which he shared with many of his contemporaries); and his promotion of Hebrew studies to facilitate an understanding of the Bible (which he shared with fellow humanists).

Erasmus had a demonstrated interest in language studies and was convinced of the importance of the word not only as a means of communication between humans but also as the medium of the divine message. Yet he does not seem to have developed a coherent philosophy of language. The mystical power of the word and its mediating function between God and human beings is an important theme in his writings, but nowhere is it presented as part of a cogent philosophical argument. In the *Lingua*, for example, Erasmus draws a parallel between the filiation of Christ and the utterance of speech. 'As the Son proceeds from the Father, so in us speech proceeds from our mind.'[46] He fails, however, to provide a rigorous argument for connecting the creative act of speaking with 'the Word being made flesh' (John 1:14). His failure is not surprising. After all, the *Lingua* is a declamation, not a philosophical dissertation. Erasmus returns to the subject in the *Ecclesiastes*. There he notes that Christ is the incarnation of the divine will and represents the mediating quality of language. The preacher's task is to use Scripture to bring Christ to his audience and to reveal the will of God. 'Preachers are the messengers of the Word of God . . . Christ is the most reliable exegete of the divine mind, never at variance with that archetype of the truth . . . Through him the eternal mind has spoken to us.'[47] Again Erasmus uses literary allusion rather than philosophical argument to express his thoughts on the power of speech.

In describing the preacher's task, Erasmus places emphasis on the mystical quality of the divine word to move and transform. On a more mundane level, he notes the psychological impact of language, its uplifting or deflating effects on the audience. In that context, too, his remarks on the relationship between word and thing, language and subject, suggest an engagement with the underlying philosophical issues. On closer analysis, however, they turn out to be no more than principles of organization. The *Method of Study*, for example, begins with a statement that appears to be informed by philosophical thought: 'Knowledge as a whole seems to be of two kinds, of things and of words. Knowledge of words comes earlier, but that of things is more important.' The statement is reminiscent of metaphysical questions raised in Plato's *Cratylus* or Aristotle's *Metaphysics*. There is, however, no follow-up connecting the statement to a body of philosophy or elaborating on its meaning. Instead, Erasmus continues with reflections on curriculum and approaches to education: 'Some people, while they hurry on to learn about things, neglect a concern for language.'[48] The distinction between words and things (that is, subject matter) forms the structural principle of Erasmus's manual of style, *De copia* (On the Abundance of Style, 1512). In the manual itself, his reflections on the relationship between words and things, however, amount to no more than comments on effective communication. Incorrect or unidiomatic usage, Erasmus says, obscures the subject. He goes as far as claiming that people lacking language skills are unable to form a proper judgement of things, but again he fails to expatiate on the philosophical implications. The distinction between words and things appears also in the prolegomena of Erasmus's New Testament edition, where he argues that speech is made up of words and things, which he likens to soul and body respectively. In the *Copia* he had used the metaphor of clothes (style) and body (thought). The philosophical intent of these metaphors remains vague, however. Erasmus's failure to anchor his comments on language in a larger framework suggests that his remarks were informed by a rhetorical rather than a philosophical impetus. Modern scholars have therefore rightly characterized his thinking on the subject as imperfectly worked out and declared that it was a futile endeavour to impute a philosophy of language to Erasmus on the basis of his scattered remarks. William Woodward noted that Erasmus's approach to the problem of semantics was typical. 'It is characteristic of him', he shrewdly observed, 'to work intuitively towards right methods whose psychological validity he had no means of proving.'[49]

By contrast, Erasmus offers readers a coherent, if traditional, educational philosophy based on pedagogical optimism. Every child has a potential waiting to be realized. 'If you do not mould your child's soul to become fully human', Erasmus warns, 'it will of itself degenerate to a monstrous bestiality.'[50] Erasmus's sentiments echo Pico della Mirandola's famous oration on the dignity of man, which postulates that all human beings have a choice between rising to a higher, quasi-divine, level or sinking to a lower, vegetative existence. Both Pico and Erasmus reflect the Christian belief that the human being was created in God's image, but is debased by sin or, as Augustine put it: 'Man's honour is the likeness of God, but his dishonour is the likeness of the beast.'[51]

Erasmus set out the principles of his educational philosophy in a tract entitled *De pueris instituendis* (On the Education of Children, 1529). Although written as a rhetorical exercise to demonstrate the treatment of a topic, first in summary, then in extended form, the work represents Erasmus's own thought on the subject and parallels views expressed elsewhere in the corpus of his writings. He describes education as a duty imposed on parents by nature as well as divine injunction. He strongly believes in the power and efficacy of instruction. In his view there is no human being that cannot benefit from education. Indeed education is what transforms us into human beings. 'Man is not born, but made man', he wrote. It was, moreover, a serious mistake to think that 'the character we are born with is all-determining'. After all, 'we can teach elephants to walk a rope, bears to dance and donkeys to perform amusing tricks. So is there anything we could not teach a human being?'[52] If children turned out evil, it was the fault of their elders who exposed them to evil rather than good influences.

Erasmus notes that excellence depends on three prerequisites: natural capacity, instruction and practice. He emphasizes that instruction is more effective than practical experience on its own. Formal teaching could accomplish 'more within the compass of a single year than the most diverse range of experience stretched over a period of 30 years'.[53] It was necessary, however, to begin education early. In support, Erasmus cites a classical commonplace: 'Farmers watch that their saplings do not grow crooked or suffer any other kind of harm . . . the sooner this is done, the more successful will be the results.' Parents shape the child from the moment of conception. They must therefore insure that procreation takes place under the most felicitous circumstances and avoid inebriation or emotional upheaval before sexual intercourse. The character of the child is formed from infancy, at first through contact with the mother. Even the quality of the breast milk fed to the child is crucial, for 'children's characters are injured by the nature of the milk as in fruits or plants the moisture of the soil changes the quality of what it nourishes'.[54] If the mother is unable to breastfeed the child herself, she must be careful in the choice of the wet nurse, who must be a sober, chaste and cheerful woman. It is important that the child hears only pure language, both in content and in enunciation. 'Nurses, teachers and playmates all make a significant contribution to the development of correct speech.' If children are exposed to slovenly or filthy language, they are bound to imitate it.[55] As soon as possible, the child should be taught the classical languages. 'This is a skill which children will acquire without any effort, whereas adults will scarcely accomplish it even with the greatest application.'[56] At the age of six, sons are to be removed from the mother's care and entrusted to their fathers or to a tutor. They must have a male model, just as daughters are expected to model themselves after their mothers.

Because humanists like Erasmus decided the dispute over the respective powers of nature and nurture in favour of the latter, they laid a heavy responsibility on the shoulders of parents and tutors. Erasmus shows that parental obligations were based both on the commands of nature and the injunctions of the Bible. Nature endowed animals with instincts, but obliged human beings to use reason as their guide. 'Nature, the mother of all things, has equipped brute animals with more means to fulfil the functions of their species; but to man alone she has given the faculty of reason, and so she has thrown the burden of human growth upon education.' What classical writers termed 'the commands of Nature', Christians saw as the design of God. Education benefited the individual and his community, but 'to speak in Christian terms, it was for God's sake and not just for themselves' that parents educated children. Erasmus reminded his readers of St Paul's words on the calling of women. They find salvation in bearing and educating their children in the ways of holiness, the apostle said. Conversely, he warned all parents that 'God would punish them for the sins of their children.'[57] Parents who educated their children well served both God and society. A well-educated child was a source of pride to his parents, 'a faithful protector of his family, a good husband to his wife and a solid and useful citizen of his country'.[58]

Acquiring knowledge and virtue were the twin purposes of education – a maxim we find in all humanistic manuals. Moral education began with the teaching of good behaviour. Small children were taught to say grace before eating and to pray at bedtime. They were told to kneel, to fold their hands in prayer and to make the sign of the cross. From such modest beginnings, they proceeded to abstract moral concepts, but 'these first-beginnings remain with them into adulthood and thus contribute in no small way to the growth of true spirituality'.[59] Given the propedeutic function Erasmus attributed to good behaviour, it is not surprising to find that he devoted a treatise to *Good Manners for Boys* (*De civilitate morum puerilium*, 1530). In presenting his advice, Erasmus once again stressed that good conduct was meaningless without motivation. His purpose in setting out rules for behaviour was 'to implant the seeds of piety in the tender heart'. He did not mean to imply that one could not be a good person without displaying good manners, but it was 'seemly for the whole man to be well ordered in mind, body, gesture and clothing'.[60]

If a father was unable to undertake the education of his sons in person, he must delegate the task to a tutor and choose a man who was knowledgeable, exemplary in his life, and equipped with the requisite pedagogical skills. The humanities must be taught humanely. The teacher of liberal studies therefore will not behave like a slave-driver. He must take into consideration the child's natural propensities and interests and present the subject matter in an attractive form, attempting to entertain and edify his young charge. Erasmus expresses horror of teachers who trust to the whip rather than to persuasion and positive reinforcement. While he usually offers commonplace arguments, his remarks on corporal punishment sound a personal note. The harsh discipline he himself experienced as a student at the Collège de Montaigu sensitized him to the suffering of children placed under the supervision of cruel masters or bullied by their classmates.[61] He inveighed against all forms of harassment and degradation, notably against 'hazing':

a practice inflicted upon students at the beginning of their studies at a public school. It is an ugly custom matched with an ugly name. Young men of good families sent to school to learn the liberal arts are subjected as part of their initiation to outrages that are unfit for human beings. First, their chins are doused as though to be shaved – and urine, or something even more disgusting, is the liquid used. This is then forced into their mouths, and they have no chance to spit it out. They are also painfully beaten, so that they may lose, as the pretence would have it, their novice's horns.[62]

Corporal punishment, Erasmus wrote, was more likely to numb a child than to motivate him, and to make him rebellious rather than compliant. It was preferable to establish a relationship of goodwill between student and master. While modern educators will approve of these sentiments, they will not entirely endorse the emphasis on competition and 'the useful spirit of rivalry' we find in Erasmus and other Renaissance pedagogues. While they disparage physical punishment, they are not averse to inflicting a measure of psychological punishment on the child by embarrassing him in front of his colleagues. 'The hope of victory and fear of disgrace will make each student more alert and eager', Erasmus notes. He adds, however, that weaker students should not be left without hope. 'Sometimes it is right to leave a pupil in the illusion that he can win even though he does not have the capacity.' [63]

In choosing a tutor a father must not show more consideration for the cost of education than for its quality. Erasmus scoffs at fathers who are more concerned with their possessions than their children. 'Each of your servants has his duties carefully assigned', he writes. 'You watch closely to whom you should give the responsibility of looking after your farm or kitchen or whom you should make your steward. But let there be one person who is quite incapable of doing anything, a lazy scoundrel and an ignorant brute, and to him you entrust the education of your child.'[64]

It will be clear from this brief survey of Erasmus educational thought that his views are conventional and do not differ appreciably from other Renaissance treatises on the subject. Indeed, readers did not look for novelty in manuals, but rather for a summary of traditional thought on the subject. Conversely, the authors of handbooks took pride in the judgement shown in their selection of commonplaces from the classics and in their presentation rather than in the originality of their thought. They referred to contemporary practices mostly for polemical purposes – to contrast the wisdom of the ancients with the folly of their own age – and introduced personal experience for the sake of piquancy or dramatic effect. Erasmus's writings fit that pattern, except that Christian philosophy is perhaps given a more prominent place in his works than in those of his Italian predecessors.

Modern readers of Erasmus's pedagogical writings may be struck by their rhetorical thrust and, in the case of *De pueris instituendis*, intent. Combining rhetoric with philosophy is, however, a hallmark of Christian humanism. Medieval writers were inclined to emphasize the dichotomy between the disciplines of rhetoric and philosophy, arguing that the truth had no need of rhetorical strategies and was in fact encumbered or debased by them. Renaissance humanists by contrast emulated classical philosophers and the early Fathers, in whose writings such a dichotomy was not apparent. Charles Trinkaus has shown that Christian humanism gave birth to a *theologia rhetorica*, a theology making use of the full range of rhetorical powers. [65] The concept can easily be transferred to Erasmus's educational writings, which might be termed a *pedagogia rhetorica*: an educational philosophy presented with rhetorical flair and argued with an arsenal of similes and metaphors.

A final observation may be in order on Erasmus's own vocation as a teacher. The progression of thought evident in his pedagogical writings suggests a broadening of his vocation over the years, from being a tutor to young men to becoming a teacher to all Christians; from teaching the Latin language to teaching the Christian life. Indeed, given the moral and religious force of Erasmus's writings, it is difficult to separate his educational philosophy from his *philosophia Christi*, which will be the focus of the next chapter.

3

Pietas in public and private life

In the catalogue of his works Erasmus designated one group of his writings as works 'teaching piety' (*quae instituunt ad pietatem*), but many if not all of his writings promote *pietas*, implicitly or explicitly. Using a vivid image, John O'Malley therefore calls piety a 'seamless robe that envelops all [Erasmus] wrote'.[1] The Erasmian concept of piety is necessarily multifaceted. Four definitions in particular are prominent in his work: piety is the correct attitude of an individual toward God and society; it is an internal quality and independent of the external observance of rites; it requires detachment from the world; and it engenders intellectual humility and an awareness of the limits of human wisdom.

Pietas, governing the proper relationship between the individual and God on the one hand, and between the individual and society on the other, is the most comprehensive definition of piety. Erasmus equates it with *caritas*, love, which flows from a sense of indebtedness to God and to fellow human beings. Charity toward one's neighbour, Erasmus says, is 'how our heavenly creditor taught us to pay our debt'.[2] In that sense, piety denotes a balance or equity and describes a relationship in which all parties give and receive their due. This concept accords with the quasi-feudal hierarchy Erasmus conceived in his *Handbook of the Christian Soldier*. Drawing on a traditional medieval image, Erasmus depicts a society arranged in three concentric circles around Christ. The clergy are closest to him, followed by the nobility and the common people. Christ occupies the centre reserved in the feudal system for the supreme overlord.[3] In Erasmus's philosophy, the image has implications for both public (or political) and private piety. At the political level, it suggests a division of tasks proper to each rank; at the spiritual level, the image is descriptive of moral authority and degrees of virtue. Erasmus allots to the clergy the duty of teaching the gospel or 'passing on' the purity of Christ, to the princes the duty of preserving peace and order, and to the people of obeying their betters and following their teaching according to their ability. Piety here resembles the Platonic virtue of justice, with each class fulfilling its duty and faithfully keeping its place.

In the *Handbook* Erasmus addresses himself primarily to the subject of personal piety. In that sense, the tiers in which he arranges society measure the distance of an individual from the moral perfection represented by Christ. Vices are beyond the pale. 'Whatever is outside the third circle is abominable, whenever and wherever it appears. In this class are ambition, love of money, lechery, anger, revenge, jealousy, slander and the other plagues.'[4] While 'every man according to the measure that is given him must strive upwards toward Christ', the clergy and the lay princes are posited closer to Christ and have a proportionately greater responsibility to imitate him and be exemplary in their conduct. Here, as in other references to social order, Erasmus insists that a high station in life must be accompanied by a heightened sense of moral responsibility. The common people, by contrast, occupy a childlike position, with a reduced level of perception and a correspondingly lower level of responsibility. Like children, they are entitled to indulgence. The clergy and nobility, cast in the paternal role with all the attendant duties, must assume leadership but also show a loving forbearance to the common people. The whole of humanity stands to God in the same relationship as the common people stand to their secular and spiritual overlords. They are children in their perception of moral virtue and must follow the lead of their Heavenly Father. 'For piety like other things has its infancy, it has its periods of growth, it has its full and vigorous adult strength', but all must strive for perfection in Christ.[5]

While the proper relationship that constitutes piety is informed here by the idea of a hierarchy, and consists in maintaining one's proper place within it, the concept of piety also applies to love between equals, or friendship. In the prefatory letter to the *Handbook* Erasmus describes the ideal monastic community as a community exemplifying piety in their life and in their thoughts and likens it to a group of friends 'banding together', 'joined willingly', and being 'of mutual service to each other'.[6] In *De contemptu mundi* (On Disdaining the World), he paints a similarly idyllic picture of the first monks as a community of friends, 'spending their time in sacred hymns, sacred literature, heavenly conversation, pious prayers'. In the early history of the institution, 'a monastery was nothing else but a congregation of men united in the true teaching of Christ . . . Friendly and brotherly scolding was the utmost punishment for them.'[7] There are striking parallels in Erasmus's description of early monasticism and the images he uses to characterize a community of friends united by a common interest for humanistic studies. He uses sacral language in speaking of their delight in literary recitals, which 'transported [them] into seventh heaven'. When one of the friends leaves the magic circle to look after his business affairs, he feels 'strangely dissatisfied . . . for leaving the Muses' sacred company to return to such profane concerns. I reflected how foolish I had been to set such store on any kind of gain as to prefer it to the holiest of pursuits.'[8] The contrast between the heavenly delights and sacred pursuits of the scholarly society on the one hand and the secular world on the other provides a conceptual link between literary and monastic communities. Both are removed from the world and consumed by love for the intangible. The spiritual and religious fervour of monks has a parallel in the aesthetic and intellectual fervour of humanists. The underlying classical notion of the poet–seer provides a subtle connection between the two callings and weaves together the concepts of friendship and piety in the sense that both are informed by a mutual obligation to serve each other in love and charity. Similar images pervade Erasmus's avowal of friendship to his pupil Thomas Grey, a young man he tutored at Paris in the 1490s. Their mutual feelings of friendship, he says, are anchored in moral and intellectual virtue. Their relationship will continue 'so long as you continue to embrace virtue and good literature'. It is a friendship that rests not on 'considerations of advantage or pleasure, or any youthful whim, but an honourable love for letters and for the studies in which we shared. Between good and studious men there is a kind of impersonal but very firm link forged by their enthusiasm for similar things.'[9]

An even closer link between intellectual friendship and piety can be found in the *Adages*, Erasmus's collection of proverbs, which begin with the saying 'Friends hold all things in common.' The adage is associated with the ancient sage Pythagoras who, Erasmus tells us, 'instituted a kind of sharing of life and property in this way, the very thing Christ wants to happen among Christians'. Erasmus equates the proper relationship between Christians (which defines piety, as we have seen) with love, for it is Christ's command to love one another that regulates the relationship between fellow Christians. In expanding on the adage 'Friends hold all things in common', Erasmus creates a direct link between Pythagoras' saying and Christ's command: 'What other purpose had Christ, the prince of our religion? One precept and one alone He gave to the world, and that was love . . . Or what else does love teach us, except that all things should be common to all?' [10] A community of friends, then, shares essential features with the ideal monastic community, which in turn exemplifies the pious fellowship of Christians. Thus Erasmus establishes a conceptual triangle between the citizens of the *res publica litteraria*, the monastic community and the Christian commonwealth. All three communities are linked by mutual goodwill and a love that transcends material interest and physical attraction – sentiments that are integral to piety.

A second important aspect of Erasmian piety is its spiritual quality. It is a state of mind rather than a type of behaviour. The *Handbook* describes the progress toward moral perfection as a progress from 'visible to invisible things', that is, a progress from the observance of rites toward perfect *pietas*, inner piety. As children of God, human beings have an obligation to develop their spiritual qualities, to live in his image and likeness.

> [The human being] participates in the visible world through the body, and in the invisible through the soul. Since we are but pilgrims in the visible world, we should never make it our fixed abode, but should relate by a fitting comparison everything that occurs to the senses either to the angelic world or, in more practical terms, to morals and to that part of man that corresponds to the angelic.[11]

Many people, however, do not rise to their higher calling. Clinging to external ceremonies instead of developing inner piety, they turn out to be superstitious rather than religious. Returning to the concept of moral growth, Erasmus emphasizes that he does not disapprove of religious ceremonies. They are, however, meant for 'infants in Christ'. Those who have reached a higher level of devotion continue to participate in these rites for the sake of those who are still at the infantile stage. The observance of rites, then, is merely a crutch, a temporary expedient, and must never be seen as an end in itself. 'To worship Christ through visible things for the sake of visible things and to think of this as the summit of religious perfection . . . would be to desert the law of the gospel, which is spiritual, and to sink into a kind of Judaism.'[12] Monks, whose calling should make them a model of piety, had sunk to the lower level in his time, Erasmus complained.

Monastic piety is everywhere cold, languid, and almost extinct because they are growing old in the letter and never take pains to learn the spiritual sense of Scriptures. They do not hear Christ crying out in the Gospel: 'The flesh is of no profit; it is the spirit that gives life', nor do they hear Paul, who adds to the words of the master: 'The letter kills, it is the spirit that gives life.[13]

In the preface to a new edition of the *Handbook of the Christian Soldier* (1518) Erasmus made the provocative statement: '*Monachatus non est pietas*' (Being a monk does not mean being pious).[14] The remark caused a great deal of indignation among members of religious orders, who interpreted it as a categorical rejection of monasticism. Erasmus rightly accused those who took offence at his comments of failing to consider their context. He pointed out that he merely stated the obvious: monastic vows did not make a person pious *ipso facto*; and monasticism was not the only road to a devout life. He offered his own definition in a polemic against the Spaniard Luis Carvajal, one of the critics who accused him of undermining respect for the monastic orders. *Pietas*, Erasmus explained, did not consist in words or actions or dress, but was 'a state of mind or disposition [*animi affectus*] encompassing love of God and love of our neighbour'.[15]

In common parlance, a member of a monastic order was called a 'religious' (*religiosus*, or pious), a usage that suggested that the monastic life was pious *per se*. Throughout the Middle Ages, the contemplative life and the cloister which signalled withdrawal from the world was regarded as the ideal life. Erasmus's attitude toward monasticism is representative of a new vision that challenged this ideal. The question whether the contemplative life was superior to the active life was raised by Petrarch in the *Secretum*, but left undecided. It was answered with a resounding 'No!' by the reformers in the sixteenth century. Erasmus's statement '*Monachatus non est pietas*' may be regarded as a milestone on the way to Luther's defiant '*Monachatus est impietas*' (The monastic life is tantamount to impiety). Some of Erasmus's readers, however, claimed that the two statements were coextensive, and that Erasmus had inspired Luther's rejection of monasticism. In his attack on the humanist, Luis Carvajal cited the popular tag 'Erasmus laid the egg, and Luther hatched the chicken', using Erasmus's statement on monasticism to prove the point. 'Luther says *Monachatus est impietas*. You say: *Monachatus non est pietas*. You see how the two of you are in agreement? But you are more destructive than Luther because you were the first to propagate this definition and publish it to the world.'[16]

This was either a gross misreading or a deliberate misrepresentation of Erasmus's words, as the humanist was quick to point out. In his writings he had expressed both admiration for exemplary monks and sharp criticism of those who betrayed the monastic ideal. He had nothing but praise for Jean Vitrier, a Franciscan, whom he set up as a model of piety to be emulated by other monks. In a short appreciation of his life, Erasmus noted that Vitrier drew his inspiration from Scripture, never looked back on the scholastics after having sampled the writings of the Fathers, and manifested the devout spirituality that springs from a mystical experience. He despised ritual as meaningless. 'It was a life for idiots rather than religious men to sleep and wake and sleep again, to speak and to be silent, to go and to return, to eat and to stop eating, all at the sound of a bell, and in a word to be governed in everything by human regulations rather than the law of Christ.' In monasteries, he said, 'men with heaven-sent gifts and born for better things were often buried by ceremonies'. In spite of such criticism, Vitrier never became an apostate or advised anyone else to abandon his vows. 'He was ready to endure everything rather than be a cause of stumbling to any mortal man.'[17] He was an excellent preacher, who could motivate others to embrace a life of piety. 'His hearers went home not only better informed, but kindled with a new desire for a pious life . . . He was absorbed by a kind of incredible passion for bringing men to the true philosophy of Christ . . . Nor were his efforts fruitless. Many were the men and women whom he had won for Christ.'[18]

Erasmus, then, gave credit where credit was due. His negative impressions of monastic piety were based on his own experience, which left him with a sour taste for the cloister and convinced him that he, at any rate, was not destined for the monastic life. His much-quoted statement on monasticism was not, however, a wholesale condemnation of religious orders. It cannot be accurately understood without taking into consideration the words that followed it and which Carvajal and other critics conveniently suppressed. The complete statement runs: 'Monasticism is not piety. It is a type of life which is either helpful or not helpful [in the pursuit of piety], depending on a person's physical and intellectual state.'[19] Thus Erasmus did not reject monasticism; he merely explained that it did not suit everyone and that it was only one of the paths leading to a pious life.

Erasmus himself took religious vows because he lacked alternatives rather than because he felt a strong vocation.[20] His essay on the advantages of the cloistered life, *De contemptu mundi* (On Disdaining the World, 1521) was written in the 1480s, shortly after he had taken vows.

It may have been an exercise in positive thinking and an effort to rational-ize the course on which he had embarked and which could not easily be reversed. The highly idealistic tract is a collection of clichés drawn mostly from a similar work of Eucherius, bishop of Lyons in the fifth century. A final chapter, added at a later time and before the date of publication,[21] qualifies the unreserved praise accorded to the monastic life in the original composition. It records Erasmus's scruples and foreshadows the sharply critical attitude toward monasticism which he adopted in the early 1520s.

In the first eleven chapters of the tract, Erasmus rehearses medieval commonplaces, depicting the monastery as a refuge from the temptations of the world, a life of prayer that lifts a man's spirit above material cares and the pleasures of the flesh. He recounts the blessings of a solitary life, free of irksome relationships, a life of composure and inner peace, and finally the sweet pleasure of contemplating heaven. In Chapter 12 by contrast, he warns young people against taking up the monastic life hastily, before they have had a chance to acquire the requisite self-knowledge. He contrasts the monasteries of his own time with the institution in its prime. Originally, he says, monasteries were indeed 'solitary dwelling places for pious men who disdained the enticements and vices that afflicted human life . . . clothed themselves humbly and ate sparingly so that any soil easily supported them'. They spent their lives in prayer and works of charity. 'In those times to be a monk meant nothing more than to be a true Christian.' In his own time, however, the monastic orders were entangled in worldly affairs and abused their privileged position. Many people now entered monasteries without vocation, either to secure a living or (as in his own case) because they had been pressured to take vows by unscrupulous parents and guardians. 'Far from preserving religious discipline [the monasteries of his time] are mere breeding places of impiety in which it is hardly possible to remain pure and innocent.'[22]

Erasmus had earlier lampooned corrupt monastic practices in the *Praise of Folly*. There he criticized the preoccupation of monks with ceremonies and the self-centredness that made them look down not only on lay people but even on other orders. 'Where has this new race of Jews sprung from?' he asked, after complaining that they did everything by rote. 'They rely so much on their ceremonies and petty man-made traditions' that they hardly regard heaven as a sufficient reward for their labours.[23] He preached against the same practices in the *Colloquies*, resorting to even more scathing criticism. In the dialogue entitled 'The Funeral' monks gather around a dying man 'like vultures' and blackmail him into bequeathing all his possessions to the Church, leaving his own family destitute. In the 'The Abbot and the Learned Lady', which has already been mentioned, an abbot openly advocates a life of pleasure and disparages learning because it might induce his monks to think critically. The 'Well-to-do Beggars' is directed against orders who lived on alms and aggressively demanded hand-outs. An innkeeper, frustrated by the brazen behaviour of the 'sons of St Francis', exclaims: 'Oh-ho, sons of St Francis, are you? You're always telling us he's a virgin, and has he so many sons?' The Franciscans explain that they are his spiritual sons. 'Unlucky begetter, he was', answers the innkeeper. 'Your spirit is the worst part of you. In body you're altogether too fit – clearly too lusty to suit one who has a wife and daughters in his house!'[24] A pair of dialogues entitled 'The Girl with No Desire to Marry' and 'The Repentant Girl' tells the story of a novice who has entered a convent against the wishes of her parents, discovers the corrupt practices followed there, repents of her decision, and makes her escape in the nick of time.

Although Erasmus was relentless in his criticism of monks who treated their profession as a sinecure, he was careful to limit his caustic remarks to those men who made a mockery of the calling. In 'The Girl with no Desire to Marry,' the protagonist anxiously replies to a young man discouraging her from entering a convent: 'Do you condemn the whole monastic life, then?' 'By no means', he answers. '[I only want to] warn all girls, particularly the talented ones, against throwing themselves rashly into something there's no escape from afterwards.'[25] Erasmus does not introduce monks merely to make them a laughing-stock. He also introduces monks that can serve as models. One character, for example, explains that he entered the Carthusian order after due consideration. 'I came to [the profession] gradually and deliberately, after self-examination and consideration of this whole system of life.' He eloquently speaks of the joys of a life consecrated to the study of the Bible and the Fathers. Conversation with such authors is delightful, he says. 'In such company, which never fails me, do you suppose solitude can become tedious?'[26]

Erasmus, whose experience was rather different from the life depicted by the Carthusian, was eventually able to free himself from the obligations he had assumed under duress. In 1516 he obtained a papal dispensation, which allowed him to reside outside the monastery and assume the dress of a secular priest. Almost immediately he came under attack from critics who claimed that he had become an apostate. They connected his initiative with Luther's disparagement of monasticism. Luther and his followers actively encouraged members of religious orders to leave their houses and materially aided them in their efforts. Erasmus never advised anyone to become an apostate. Explaining his own situation, he contended that he had not been a monk in the proper sense of the word. It was 'voluntary profession' (*spontanea confessio*) that made a man a monk; his own profession had been forced. Nevertheless he had not run away, as some of his enemies claimed, but had left the monastery and changed his dress 'with the formal approval of [his] superiors' (*authoritate maiorum*). [27]

The desire to distance himself from the reformers may have prompted Erasmus to adopt more moderate language concerning monasticism in the late 1520s. In a letter to an unidentified monk, who had asked him for advice, he counselled him to remain in the cloister and to beware of the 'evangelical freedom' promised by the reformers. He regretted that his earlier criticism of the monastic orders had been misinterpreted: 'I wished for a little curtailment of ceremonies and a great increase in true piety, but now ceremonies are abandoned in such a way that instead of spiritual freedom we have uncontrolled carnal licence.' He returned to the phrases he had used in *Disdaining the World*, describing monastic life as 'a taste, as it were, of the blessed life in heaven'.[28] His changed perspective also led Erasmus to revise the *Handbook* for an edition published in 1529. Although he refused to alter the controversial statement that monasticism did not constitute piety, he added a quotation from Jerome, who called monastic orders 'the most precious jewel among the adornments of the Church'.[29] He then called on the religious orders to live up to the Church Father's praise. The following year, Erasmus published a psalm commentary, in which he further clarified his position. He distinguished between the institution and its members, between the ideal and its realization. He approved of the ideal, which he said represented 'the sum of heroic virtues', and which was realized by those 'who are truly dead to the world and have given themselves completely to God'. The monastic community that achieved this ideal was indeed 'the image of the city of God'. Erasmus counselled his readers to respect the institution and overlook those who perverted the ideal. 'If we hate the good because of the bad, we cannot approve of any kind of life . . . [We must] interpret what is doubtful in the best possible light, wink at lesser faults, try to remedy rather than exasperate the more severe faults, and respect the order and institution itself.'[30]

Erasmus's concept of piety, then, focused on spiritual qualities, of which pious actions were merely an extension. Thus he did not share the reformers' disdain for 'works' but adopted a typically Catholic point of view, which saw the observance of ceremonies as supplementary and, where required by Church law, obligatory. Contrary to the Lutheran doctrine of 'faith alone' (*sola fide*), Erasmus maintained the Catholic position that both faith and works were needed to obtain salvation.

Docta pietas, a catchphrase repeatedly used by Erasmus,[31] describes a third aspect of his concept: the intellectual dimension of piety, which underlies Christian scholarship. St Jerome was the man who exemplified *docta pietas* for Erasmus. In his *Life of Jerome*, the first attempt to replace hagiography with a critical biography, Erasmus described his gifts as 'a mingling of all the supreme qualities' that characterize the Christian scholar. He equalled Cicero in the brilliance of his expression. At the same time, he had a thorough knowledge of Scripture, and everywhere in his writings breathed the spirit of Christ. Who could match this paragon of Christian scholarship, 'either for holiness of life or for mastery of theology?'[32]

The opposite of *docta pietas* is *impia curiositas*: unholy curiosity. Erasmus warns against it in the *Ratio*, his curriculum for theology students. He counsels students to be zealous in their pursuit of the truth, but to avoid undue speculation. *Docta pietas*, the intellectual virtue of the Christian scholar, includes a respect for 'sacred limits'. The would-be theologian must approach learning humbly, and avoid 'pertinacity, the parent of strife'. He does not arrogantly trust his own judgement, but waits patiently for the Holy Spirit to enlighten him. 'Embrace what you are allowed to perceive', Erasmus writes, 'venerate from afar what you are not allowed to perceive, and look in awe and with simple faith on whatever it is that is concealed from you. Keep far away from impious curiosity.'[33] While intellectual curiosity is encouraged in our own time and regarded as a desirable quality, it was viewed with suspicion in Erasmus's time. *Curiositas* invariably denoted an unwarranted degree of intellectual curiosity, especially prying into or quibbling about sacred matters. It was the principal fault Erasmus found in scholastic exegetes, who attempted to explain and explore what he regarded as holy mysteries.

In the Erasmian scheme of things, knowledge and learning are neutral qualities, which become good or evil, depending on their focus. We have seen that Erasmus placed Christ at the centre of his social and political system. One of the rules he established in his *Handbook of the Christian Soldier* was 'Place Christ before you as the only goal of your life.' The usefulness of learning was measured by this rule.

You love the study of letters? Good, if it is for the sake of Christ. If you love it only in order to have knowledge, then you come to a standstill at a point from which you should have gone on. But if you are interested in letters so that with their help you may more clearly discern Christ . . . then, having discerned him, may love him, and by knowing and loving him, may communicate this knowledge and delight in it, then gird yourself for the study of letters. Yet do not allow it to go beyond what you think will be profitable to your virtuous intent.[34]

Here we have in a nutshell Erasmus's concept of learned piety. It flows from his general definition of piety as love of God and humanity. It has a social dimension: communicating our love to the world around us. And it must respect certain limits, beyond which knowledge becomes un-profitable or even sinful. In circumscribing the usefulness of pagan learning, for example, Erasmus frequently uses the simile of 'spoiling the Egyptian' to denote the process of taking from the classics what was useful, of Christianizing pagan learning.[35] 'Spoiling the Egyptian' could also mean applying secular learning to a sacred purpose and using it to promote spirituality. Christian scholarship requires the translation of knowledge into moral practice. It is in this point that Erasmus's definition of piety as love of God and fellow human beings merges with his definition of Christian scholarship. By living well and 'deserving well of all men', the scholar uses his gospel learning and allows his life to serve as testimony to God's word. His life becomes 'a sacred sermon'. The first step is to learn (*scire*) the philosophy of Christ, the second is to practise it (*praestare*).[36]

The major point in Erasmus's criticism of scholastic theologians is their failure to convert their learning into pious action. In his opinion, the scholastic curriculum divorced scholarship from ethics. It was barren because it was inapplicable to the Christian life. In their hands, 'the sacred discipline of theology had been turned into something sophistic'. Jerome, by contrast, was a true representative of the sacred discipline. He mastered the 'whole cycle of knowledge in its completeness, and in a wonderful harmony blended with it the full circle of a bishop's virtues'. Thus he manifested *docta pietas*, which combined intellectual with moral excellence: 'Who had a more thorough knowledge of the philosophy of Christ? Who expressed it more forcefully in his writings and in his life?'[37]

It is an Erasmian feature that he treats the same theme in different literary forms, as if he were experimenting with genres to discover the best medium for the message. While professional philosophers usually consider a systematic approach the best way of instructing the reader, Erasmus seems to aim for the same effect through repetition and variation. Although the *Handbook* is the most important source for his concept of piety, it must be read in conjunction with his satire, *The Praise of Folly* (1511). As we have seen, that work offers important insights into Erasmus's thoughts on piety. At first glance it seems to have little in common with the devotional treatise, but Erasmus himself tips us off to the connection between the two works. Defending the *Folly* against the criticism of theologians, who decried it as frivolous and disrespectful, Erasmus wrote: 'The *Folly* is concerned in a playful spirit with the same subject as the *Handbook of the Christian Soldier*. My purpose was guidance and not satire; to help, not to hurt; to show men how to become better and not stand in their way.' Adopting a playful tone, he hoped to insinuate himself into his readers' hearts, 'and not only cure them but amuse them too. I had often observed that this cheerful and humorous style of putting people right is with many of them most successful.'[38] In the *Folly* Erasmus adopts what appears to be a light-hearted thesis: being foolish means being happy. He 'proves' his thesis with numerous examples: foolish lovers overlook the faults of their beloved; foolish poets are unaware of the mediocrity of their compositions; foolish teachers enjoy a sense of power, lording it over a troop of schoolchildren; foolish scholastic theologians take pride in their useless learning. After mercilessly lampooning the foibles of humanity without regard for social rank or professional prestige, Erasmus comes to a surprising and, at first blush, paradoxical conclusion: fools will be rewarded with heavenly bliss. Unfolding the paradox, he explains that those who pay no attention to worldly matters or value spiritual wealth more highly than monetary gain are often regarded as fools. Their situation is much like that of the man in Plato's cave, who has seen the sun and no longer values shadows. He now pities his former companions and deplores their ignorance, while they in turn regard him as a madman. Similarly, 'the pious scorn whatever concerns the body and are wholly uplifted towards the contemplation of invisible things'. Rising above physical considerations, they are 'beside' themselves, or in ecstasy.

> And so when the whole man will be outside himself, and happy for no reason except that he is so outside himself, he will enjoy some ineffable share in the supreme good which draws everything into itself . . . The life of the pious is no more than a contemplation and foreshadowing of that other life, at times they are able to feel some foretaste and savour of

the reward to come . . . So those who are granted a foretaste of this –
and very few have the good fortune – experience something which is
very like madness.[39]

The fact that the *Praise of Folly* is not merely a lampoon, but a channel for
Erasmus's thoughts on piety is no doubt a factor in its continued appeal.
The concept of piety presented here can be grasped by readers today as in
Erasmus's time, whereas the topical wit directed against the peccadilloes
and corrupt practices of his own time require a historical commentary to
be fully understood. Erasmus, then, successfully used satire as a vehicle
to communicate his idea of piety. He employed dialogue with similar skill
and to the same purpose. The *Colloquies* were, in their modest first
edition, no more than a handful of short dialogues to teach schoolboys
Latin. The book went through numerous editions and additions. The
added dialogues changed its nature and transformed it from a manual of
instruction into a vehicle of social criticism. In its new form, the book
attracted considerable criticism from theologians, who declared that it
was unsuitable for boys and, furthermore, contained blasphemies – not to
say heresies. Erasmus was therefore obliged to append, in 1529, an essay
'On the Usefulness of the *Colloquies*', in which he defended himself
against such accusations. He insisted that the book contained salutary
lessons in moral philosophy, although not in the usual systematic form. 'I
don't think I should be reproached for attracting youth with like zeal to
refinement of Latin speech and to good conduct', he wrote. Using the
opportunity to strike out against the scholastics, he added: 'Aristotle's
Ethics is not suited to boys, the theology of Scotus still less – it's not of
much use even for improving the minds of grown men – but to implant
from the start a taste for excellence in young minds is urgent.'[40]

After these preliminary remarks, Erasmus turns to the defence of
individual dialogues, describing in a few strokes their moral purpose. The
various aspects of his concept of piety are well represented. The opinion
that the monastic life does not exemplify piety and is not necessarily the
best way to learn piety is the subject of three dialogues. 'The Girl with No
Interest in Marriage' and 'The Repentant Girl' have already been
mentioned. The same theme appears also in 'The Whole Duty of Youth',
a kind of catechism. A precocious young man discusses the meaning of
religion. His interlocutor suggests that it is exemplified by monasticism:
'If I wanted to be religious I'd put on a cowl.' 'So would I', answers the
young man, 'if a cowl provided as much piety as warmth'.[41] Other
warnings about taking religious vows follow. Critics feared that Erasmus's

candid words of warning would deter aspirants to the monastic life. 'Maybe there will [be fewer monks] but better ones', Erasmus answers. 'Any monk worthy of the name will back me on that.'[42] In several dialogues, Erasmus condemned the mechanical observance of rites and emphasized that piety was a spiritual quality. In the 'Profane Feast', a group of friends at dinner discuss fasting and other regulations. Answering critics of the colloquy, Erasmus explained that he did not intend to disparage the laws of the Church concerning fasting and choices of food. He merely wished to expose 'the superstition of certain persons who attach excessive importance to these matters while neglecting those that contribute more to godliness . . . likewise the absurd holier-than-thou attitude of those who condemn their neighbour on such grounds.'[43] Super-stition masquerading as piety is also lampooned in 'The Spectre', in which a charlatan stages apparitions of demons and heavenly messengers, and in 'A Pilgrimage for Religion's Sake', in which the priorities of people are questioned, who spend their money on travel and on indul-gences granted at shrines instead of looking after their families. As in the *Handbook of the Christian Soldier*, Erasmus emphasizes that he does not condemn ceremonies and rites, and is willing to concede much to people's whims, 'but for these people to arrogate piety to themselves from all this is intolerable'. It is more important to warn of superstitious practices and point out the difference between external and internal piety than it is to denounce manifest sins such as gluttony or adultery. 'The danger to true piety comes rather from evils that are not perceived or that entice in the guise of righteousness.'[44] Touching as they do on the various aspects of righteousness, the *Colloquies* thus provide a good introduction to Erasmus's concept of piety.

In his apologetic essay, Erasmus justifies his use of different genres to teach ethics. Using humour to inculcate virtue may strike the stern theolo-gians as unorthodox, but people differ in nature and are 'drawn to piety by a thousand means'.

Augustine disputes, Jerome contends in dialogues, Prudentius wars in various forms of verse, Thomas and Scotus fight with the help of dialectic and philosophy. All have the same purpose, but each uses a different method. Variety is not condemned so long as the same goal is sought. Peter of Spain is taught to boys to prepare them the more readily for proceeding to Aristotle. One who instils a liking for something does much. And this little book, if taught to ingenuous youth, will lead them to many more useful studies: to poetry, rhetoric, physics, ethics, and finally to matters of Christian piety.[45]

In spite of this spirited defence, Erasmus's *Colloquies* were one of his first writings to be placed on the Index of Forbidden Books.[46] In a way, the effort of Church authorities to suppress the dialogues was an acknowledgement of their effectiveness as a teaching tool. At the same time it was a rejection of the corrosive nature of Erasmus's criticism and an expression of fear that his emphasis on invisible things would undermine the authority of the visible, institutional Church. Indeed, although Erasmus's concept of piety is too complex to be reduced to one phrase, his principal message seems to be that piety exists independently of the conventions and articles that make an institutional Church.

4

Princes, popes and people: The social order

Hierarchical order is the principle that informs Erasmus's definition of piety as well as his views on the best organization of society. Like many Renaissance ideals, it had both classical and Christian roots. It was modelled on the heavenly kingdom of God and on the ancient notion that monarchy was the best form of government.[1] The hierarchical principle prevailed in utopian fiction from Plato's republic to More's island. The ideal society was tiered, tightly regulated and controlled from above.

The desirability of maintaining the status quo was another enduring shibboleth. Tradition was regarded as a validating principle in antiquity as well as in Erasmus's time. In classical Latin, the idiom *cupidus rerum novarum*, literally 'desirous of new things', had a negative connotation, describing a rebellious individual. Until the eighteenth century, therefore, social and political critics shied away from portraying themselves as innovators. Instead, they claimed to be the defenders of traditional ideals, which had been corrupted in the course of time. Invariably, their professed aim was a return to the original, pristine state. Renaissance society, then, was anchored in the trinity of law, order and tradition. Hierarchical order provided the framework, tradition supplied the justification for this order and laws ensured its continuity. This was the bedrock on which social and political relationships rested. It defined not only the relationship between ruler and subject, but also that of parent and child, husband and wife and, ultimately, God and the believer.

The institutional bias of Renaissance society in favour of the status quo is reflected in the genre called the Mirror of Princes, which usually depicts a stable and harmonious relationship between ruler and ruled. Machiavelli is exceptional in acknowledging their distinct and sometimes opposing interests. In his *Il Principe* (*The Prince*, 1513) he therefore proclaims the need for clever management or brutal force to maintain the status quo. In devising his policies – domestic or foreign – the Machiavellian prince is motivated by self-interest. More typically, however, the authors of Renaissance Mirrors were idealists. The princes they depicted ruled for the common good. As Machiavelli himself noted, the majority of the manuals described 'imagined states and principalities that nobody ever saw or knew in the real world'. The authors were concerned not with the existing state of things but with 'the way we ought to live'.[2] Most of Erasmus's political writings are of the kind deprecated by Machiavelli. They are prescriptive rather than analytical, and charged with a moral imperative. Erasmus goes so far as to suggest that a prince who cannot live up to the established ideal should abdicate.[3] While Machiavelli illustrates his theories with a plethora of examples drawn from recent history, Erasmus's references to contemporary affairs and conditions existing in his time are largely restricted to two areas: the politics of war and peace and the threat of a religious schism. These are subjects that preoccupied Erasmus and prompted him to offer political comment, as opposed to political theory. In other areas, however, Erasmus was too discreet or too cautious to refer to specific persons or events. When he proposed political actions that were at variance with popular opinion or experience, he often presented them in a historical context and cited classical or biblical sources in their support. Thus he introduced the idea of electing a territorial prince as a 'custom among some barbarian peoples in the past'. To illustrate voluntary abdication, he used the example of the legendary Codrus of Athens, and in support of the idea of ruling by consensus, he cited Xenophon.[4]

Although Erasmus frequently reflects on politics, his remarks are often incidental or peripheral to other subjects. I will therefore limit my discussion to three themes that recur frequently in his writings and receive more than episodic attention: the hierarchical arrangement of society; the desirability of peace; and the relationship between state and Church.

HIERARCHICAL ORDER

The main source for Erasmus's political thought is the *Institutio principis christiani* (The Education of a Christian Prince, 1515), but one of the most important passages on hierarchical order appears in the prefatory letter to the second edition of his *Handbook of the Christian Soldier* (1518). I have already described the image used by Erasmus there: the three circles, which establish a hierarchy by proximity to the central figure of Christ and the ideals he represents. This hierarchy is divinely instituted and governs both the secular and the spiritual world. 'Just as God wished that there should be order among the members of his own body . . . so in the whole commonwealth in which there are both good and evil, he wished that there be a certain order.' Since this order is instituted by divine will, those who disturb it 'fight against God, its author'.[5]

In the image of the three estates surrounding Christ in concentric circles, the second tier is assigned to princes. In speaking of the qualities and powers of the prince, Erasmus establishes a parallel between the secular and the spiritual world. Philosophers are agreed, he says, 'that the most healthy [constitutional] form is monarchy; not surprisingly, for by analogy with the deity, when the totality of things is in one person's power, then indeed, in so far as he is in this respect in the image of God, he excels everyone else in wisdom and goodness'. The ideal ruler then is just, wise and good, embodying the qualities of the divine king. Similarly, his relationship to the subjects of his realm is modelled on the relationship between God and the believer. The good ruler is a father to his subjects, a model of goodness, an equitable judge and, like Christ, a 'prince of peace'. Conversely, the subjects owe him and his legal representatives unquestioning obedience, as they would to God. The parallel ends there, however. God is always just; secular princes are human and subject to vices. Even so, 'they must be honoured where they perform their duty and put up with perhaps where they use their power for their own advantage, lest something worse arise in their place'.[6] The unnamed evil Erasmus fears is chaos and anarchy. 'Since the public order cannot be firm unless authority is granted to the magistrates, you too should obey them for the sake of the common need of the state', Erasmus counsels citizens. Even if rulers are impious and unjust, 'nevertheless, because they administer public justice and because God is justice, they are the ministers of God and in a way rule for him as long as they apply their efforts to the mandate given them by public authority'.[7]

Justifying the need for a hierarchical order, Erasmus relied on the same arguments and used the same illustrations as his ancient and medieval predecessors. The social organization of bees and ants were favourite points of reference.[8] Exemplified in nature, hierarchical order was regarded as the guarantor of peace and the basis of civilization. 'Order', Erasmus wrote, 'is a good in itself.'[9] Conversely, a lack of understanding for the order of society and, more generally, of the ranking that informed it, was an evil. *Praeposterum iudicium* (inverted or perverted judgement) was the ruin of morals and of the commonwealth. If the natural order was reversed and affairs of state were controlled by the 'foolishness of the people' rather than the 'wisdom of the prince', it would be as preposterous and ruinous as if the mind were controlled by the body.[10] To give the idea of a hierarchical order more authority, Erasmus cites Plato among the ancients and Dionysius the Areopagite among his medieval followers. The hierarchical scheme he proposes reflects both Plato's ranking, in which the guardians are placed at the head of society and directed to rule for the good of the community, and even more closely the order devised by Dionysius in his *Ecclesiastical Hierarchy*. He cites him for the triple ranking: 'What God is in the ranks of heaven, the bishop should be in the Church and the prince in the state.'[11] To justify order in the state, Erasmus offers a series of traditional analogies, classical and Christian. A hierarchically ordered society paralleled the control of the mind over the body, of reason over emotion and of God's rule over creation.[12]

Since the prince's position is superior to that of his subjects, his mind and his conduct must be superior as well. Principalities in Erasmus's time were hereditary. It followed that education played a paramount role in developing the prince's potential and raising him to the desired level of accomplishment. Plato furnished the model for Erasmus's philosopher-king. 'Unless you are a philosopher you cannot be a prince, only a tyrant', Erasmus writes, in order to justify his demand for a thorough training in ethics which will teach the prince that 'virtue is its own great reward'. He cites Aristotle's *Politics* for another criterion distinguishing the prince from the tyrant: 'The latter is concerned for his own interests and the former for the state'.[13] By virtue of his position as steward of God, the prince must be morally superior not only to his people but also generally to non-Christians. 'Crude power and dominion are pagan terms', Erasmus says. The authority of a Christian prince, by contrast, rests on merit. His rule amounts to 'administration, benefaction and guardianship'.[14]

Although Erasmus frequently resorted to classical examples to illustrate and give weight to his views, he expected a Christian prince to surpass his pagan predecessors in moral excellence. Erasmus addressed the *Education of the Christian Prince* to 15-year-old Prince Charles, who was then the ruler of the Low Countries, but within a year succeeded to the Spanish throne and three years later (in 1519) was invested with the imperial crown. Erasmus coupled his advice to the prince with a translation of similar advice written by the Greek orator Isocrates for the ancient Cyprian king Nicocles. In his prefatory letter, Erasmus stressed the difference between the respective authors and their addressees.

Isocrates 'was a sophist instructing some petty king or rather tyrant, and both were pagans; I am a theologian addressing a renowned and upright prince, Christians both of us.' He noted the implications: 'You should be as different from even the noble pagan princes as a Christian is from a pagan.'[15] Erasmus's description of the ideal prince therefore draws on numerous biblical examples in addition to the classical models.[16]

The prince's position in the state is akin to that of the paterfamilias, the head of the family. The same principle of hierarchy that informs society and the relationship between subject and ruler therefore also applies to the family and the relationship between father and children. The father and the prince think alike:

> Whatever gain comes to any member of the family represents an increase in his own fortunes, so he who is endowed with a princely spirit thinks of any possessions which his subjects have anywhere as being part of his own wealth; for he has them so devoted and dedicated to himself that they do not shrink from anything, even from laying down their lives, not just their money, for the prince.[17]

There is little need to document the fact that Erasmus subscribes to the notion (enforced in his time by secular and canon law) that children are subject to the parental will in all major life decisions. It is more to the point to document where and to what extent he diverges from that norm. We have already seen that he places emphasis on the humane element in the relationship between ruler and subject and between parent (or tutor) and child, and that he wants command and obedience informed by reciprocal love and devotion. While a father may be within his right to chastize his son or to dictate his profession, the humane father uses other means of motivation and takes into consideration the son's interests and inclinations. While he may be within his rights to choose a husband for his daughter, he will take into consideration her own wishes and desires.

In his *Colloquies* Erasmus draws on a number of scenarios that illustrate the difference between parental justice and equity, the rights granted them by law and usage and the concessions made to family members out of affection. In 'A Marriage in Name Only' (1529) Erasmus decries the practice of parents marrying off their daughter to a man on account of the suitor's wealth or social status and without consideration for his moral or physical suitability for becoming the lifelong partner of their daughter. Erasmus made that point also in his principal work on marriage, *Institutio matrimonii* (The Institution of Marriage, 1526), denouncing parents 'who will hand over a pure and healthy virgin to a husband riddled with the new leprosy [syphilis]'. After all, the principal purpose of marriage, according to the Church and sixteenth-century sensibilities, was procreation. 'Why should a marriage made with a man incapable of sexual intercourse be annulled, and yet a contract be valid with a man who produces pus instead of semen and begets pox instead of children?'[18] If syphilis was the consequence of an earlier sexual indiscretion, it pointed not only to a diseased body but also to a flawed character in the groom. The daring nature of Erasmus's suggestion that the disease should be ground for a divorce becomes evident when contrasted with an anecdote in a contemporary handbook, *De institutione feminae christianae* (On the Education of the Christian Woman) by Juan Luis Vives. Like Erasmus, Vives touches on the subject of a young woman's marriage to an old syphilitic man. The point of his example, however, is to exemplify the virtue of loyalty under all circumstances. Far from resenting her partner, the wife in Vives' narrative devotes her life to nursing her diseased husband. Vives' ideal no doubt represents mainstream thought, as evidenced by the positive reception of Boccaccio's famous story of Griselda's martyrdom. The moral is the same: a wife is expected to love and serve her husband regardless of the treatment she receives at his hands. Erasmus himself is well aware of the appeal of melodramatic stories and makes clever use of them in his colloquy 'Marriage' (1526) – not to endorse the traditional message but to examine it. The protagonists in the dialogue are named 'Eulalia' (Well-spoken) and 'Xanthippe' (i.e. the proverbial shrew). Eulalia, who plays marriage counsellor to Xanthippe, urges her to be more compliant and submissive to her husband. She tells two anecdotes to illustrate the point. In the first a recalcitrant young bride is cowed into submission by a menacing father and lives happily ever after. In the other, a model wife supplies a soft bed and gourmet dinners to her husband's mistress to ensure that he will not be deprived of the comforts of home. The examples are supposed to inspire Xanthippe to show similar goodwill and bear with her husband who is a womanizer and a tippler. Since Eulalia represents the 'correct' view, one would expect acquiescence from Xanthippe. Erasmus, however, breaks with the tradition of didactic literature. Xanthippe reacts critically and declares the two 'success stories' unconvincing. 'Too good a wife!' she exclaims in response to the second story. 'I'd sooner have made him a bed of nettles and thistles . . . I'd rather die than be bawd to my husband.'[19] Throughout the dialogue, Erasmus skilfully negotiates between the 'good' advice of Eulalia and the 'bad' behaviour of Xanthippe. He provides a level playing field by giving Xanthippe witty, commonsense lines, while Eulalia, the paragon of wives, comes across as saccharine and hypocritical. This nuancing of roles suggests that Erasmus did not want his readers to see the situation in black and white. His purpose is to recommend accommodation rather than confrontation, equity rather than justice.

In the 'Courtship' he shows a similar tendency to manoeuvre between the lines. In that dialogue a suitor proposes to the young woman he loves. He is clearly respectable and depicted as holding the 'correct' views on the roles of husband and wife. In one point, however, he is rather unconventional. He expects his lover to make her own decision: 'I say "I am yours"; you chime in with "I am yours."' The young woman, by contrast, is conservative, insisting that he must obtain her parents' consent. She asks her suitor to speak to them first: 'I'm not a free agent . . . I think our marriage will have more chance of success if it's arranged by our parents' authority.' [20] Thus Erasmus acknowledges the legal and conventional power of parents to make such decisions. At the same time he shows awareness of the changing mores of his time. No warning note is sounded. The unconventional young man is not depicted as a dangerous seducer who wants to lead an innocent young woman astray. He is depicted as a desirable suitor likely to make a good husband. Thus Erasmus creates the expectation that the parents will respect the wishes of the young couple, but does not go as far as saying that they should leave the choice to them entirely.

The hierarchical principle, then, applies to the family as it does to society as a whole. In both cases, however, Erasmus recommends tempering the rigour of the law. His emphasis on equity rather than cold justice should not be construed as a move to weaken the hierarchical order but rather as an attempt to distinguish between law and application, general principle and individual case. Recommending leniency in individual cases does not constitute an abrogation of the law or the principle in question. An interesting comment on the need for a father to be, or at any rate to appear, a stern disciplinarian shows the value Erasmus put on the principle. Discussing a passage in Sirach counselling fathers to be severe and 'never let their daughters see them smile', he interjects:

What kind of advice is this? How can a father not love his daughters, especially if they are dutiful and God-fearing, and, if he loves them, how can he look upon them with an unsmiling face? But in fact, if you truly love your daughters, that is why you will hide your smiles when you see them. Where is the danger? It is important that girls of that age should always be constrained by feelings of respect, and too much cheerfulness in the father's face will detract from this not a little. If his daughters do something unbecoming they are rebuked by a stern glance from their father; if they have done nothing wrong, their father's expression must still be serious (but not harsh) to remind them not to err.[21]

The father is an authority figure in the hierarchical order of society; he must stay in character to support that order. One concludes that Erasmus's recommendation of equity stopped well short of questioning the principle of order in society.

In Erasmus's time the authorities of Church and state overlapped, sometimes placing morally conflicting demands on individuals. It is not surprising therefore that Erasmus shows some ambivalence in discussing the obligations of children to their natural and their spiritual parent respectively. In *Disdaining the World*, he praises the behaviour of a young woman who disobeys her parents and enters a monastery. Conversely, he disparages the behaviour of the parents, who oppose her spiritual quest. Thus he signals to the reader that the young woman's vocation is a gift of God. The commands of God, her spiritual father, supersede the commands of her earthly parents. In the *Colloquies*, by contrast, Erasmus develops a narrative in which parents object to their daughter entering a convent. The events prove them right. The young woman is depicted as foolish and headstrong; the parents as serving the best interests of their daughter. The two narratives may demonstrate that complex questions must be settled case by case and cannot be governed by one rule. In one case the vocation is genuine and the parents have no right to interfere; in the other it is a young girl's fancy and the parents have an obligation to interfere. Alternatively the two stories may serve as a warning to historians and point out the difficulty of extrapolating Erasmus's views from literary genres that are notoriously difficult to interpret. *On Disdaining the World* is a protreptic; the *Colloquies* are dialogues. These genres are not reliable indicators of an author's views since they permit adopting a pose for the sake of exercising one's ingenuity or to further the storyline. Finally, it is worth noting that the ambivalence concerning parental authority is present also in the Bible, the sourcebook of Christian morality. The commandment 'Honour thy father and thy mother' is qualified by Christ's rejection of earthly concerns ('No one is worthy of me who cares more for his father and mother than for me') and his warning: 'I have come to set a man against his father.'[22]

An examination of Erasmus's comments on the proper relationship between husband and wife presents similar difficulties of interpretation. Erasmus's overall message is that the law makes the wife subject to the husband, but love makes the relationship equitable. In the colloquy 'Courtship', the young suitor therefore describes husband and wife as joint rulers of the household: 'I will be your king, you will be my queen.' Elsewhere, Erasmus uses the image of body and soul to describe the relationship between wife and husband. The simile is suggestive of the traditional superiority of the male over the female, but Erasmus softens the implications when he elaborates: 'The spirit is the greater of the two, but it is for the body's benefit; the spirit does not dominate and overwhelm it, but makes concessions to assist it.'[23] In the 'New Mother', which has already been mentioned, a woman challenges the idea of male supremacy and is given all the winning lines by Erasmus. The male interlocutor, Eutrapelus, rehearses a number of traditional arguments in favour of male superiority. The man has greater strength, he says. He has been created first, has been made the 'head' of the woman and is the defender of his country. The female antagonist, Fabulla, parries each argument. Camels are stronger than man, she argues, but this does not prove their superiority. Artists usually improve, thus their mature work is better than their early work. If man is the 'head of woman', she is the 'glory of man', and besides, both have been created in the image of God and are members of the mystical body of Christ. Men may excel women in physical endowments, but women excel men in spiritual gifts. 'In which sex is there more drunkenness, more brawls, fights, killings, wars, robberies and adulteries?' she asks. Undeniably men were more liable to commit these crimes and misdemeanours. Finally, childbirth is more dangerous than going into battle to defend the country. 'There's not a single man who, if he once experienced childbirth, would not prefer standing in a battle line ten times over.' Thus ends the disputation, but Erasmus keeps his tongue firmly in cheek, suggesting that the question does not admit of a magisterial solution.[24]

While Erasmus sees room for negotiation between unmarried daughters and parents and between wife and husband, he is rather conservative in his views on the status of widows. The desire for order is at the bottom of Erasmus's recommendation that a young widow remarry. Freedom from the authority of a husband is a dangerous thing and an undesirable condition. The young widow may abuse her newfound freedom and waste her time on frivolities or worse. For 'these evils marriage is the remedy. The authority of a husband will bring the natural levity occasioned by his wife's youth and sex under control; then too the responsibilities of a family give little space to idleness.'[25] The alternative is entering a convent, which, like marriage, provides for a structured life. Erasmus adds the usual caution, however: this important choice should not be made rashly and without a vocation. Hierarchy, then, governs Erasmus's thought on social and political relationships. It is the guarantor of order and stability. Yet he never praises the advantages of a hierarchical structure without warning of its inherent dangers: tyranny and abuse of authority.

WAR AND PEACE

Nowhere is the risk of abuse greater than in power politics and its collateral, armed conflict. The conditions under which a ruler should resort to warfare are a frequent topic of discussion in Erasmus's political writings. In this context he introduces the idea of a limited monarchy. The concept of checking the prince's powers in general and his power to declare war in particular can be found in classical sources such as Aristotle's *Politics*.[26] Erasmus's source of inspiration may have been closer at hand, however. The political practices in his homeland furnished an example. In Brabant, the prince's authority was traditionally limited by a council, and the position of Prince Charles and his father Philip the Fair *vis-à-vis* the estates may be reflected in Erasmus's statement that 'the monarchy should preferably be checked and diluted with a mixture of aristocracy and democracy to prevent it ever breaking out into tyranny; and just as the elements mutually balance each other, so let the state be stabilized with a similar control'.[27] The statement can be explained equally well as a reference to classical political theory or to the contemporary debate over the power of the estates in Brabant. Similar considerations apply to Erasmus's suggestion that there should be a consensus between prince and people on important political decisions. He presents the idea in a historical context, citing Xenophon on 'ruling the people with their consent' rather than treating them like slaves.[28] Yet his statement that 'government depends to a large extent on the consent of the people, which was what created kings in the first place'[29] may equally well reflect traditions and beliefs nearer to his own time. In 1484, for example, Philippe Pot noted that according to French tradition, 'kings were originally created by the votes of the sovereign people'. The idea that political authority was derived 'from the common consent and election of the community' (as Duns Scotus put it) was supported by a number of prominent medieval writers, with whose works Erasmus would have been familiar.[30] Erasmus notes that disagreements between rulers were less likely to end in military combat if they were required to seek the consent of their subjects before going to war.

Recent history may also have suggested another expedient mentioned by Erasmus as an alternative to war: arbitration. 'If some dispute arises between princes, why do they not take it to arbitration instead?' he asks. There was no need for bloodshed when the question could be resolved by the authority of popes, bishops or other men of authority. Indeed, it was 'the proper function of the Roman pontiff . . . to settle disputes between Christian princes'.[31] Arbitration was a frequent means of settling disputes in the fourteenth and fifteenth centuries. It was used more often among cities and lesser principalities than among the greater powers, but the Treaty of Tordesillas (1494) provided an important model for the latter. The settlement of boundaries between the colonial empires of Spain and Portugal through the agency of Pope Alexander VI no doubt left an impression on Erasmus. His demand for consensus and consultation, then, was fed by both classical and contemporary examples. Finally, we may regard Erasmus's insistence on consensus as an aspect of his episte-mology, which will concern us in more detail in Chapter 6. Briefly put, Erasmus was well practised in the *ars dubitandi*, the examination of both sides of an issue. Originating in the classical sceptical tradition, this method called for the suspension of judgement if an issue was too complex to be settled by reasoning. Later sceptics allowed for a settlement based on probability. The scholastic method of *sic et non*, which was the medieval version of argumentation on both sides, settled such questions by a magisterial decision. In matters concerning articles of faith Erasmus himself took refuge in the magisterial decisions of the Church, but in other matters he proposed to use consensus as a decision-making tool or to submit contentious issues to the verdict of respected authorities.

Apart from the *Education of the Christian Prince*, the declamation *The Complaint of Peace* and the adage 'War is sweet to those who do not know it' are prominent sources for Erasmus's thoughts on war and peace. The two pieces have remained popular through the ages and have been frequently reprinted and translated, but they are rhetorical in nature and therefore more appealing as manifestos of humanitarian thought than as political theory. Erasmus's psalm commentaries turn out to be a better source, since his political ideas are anchored in the teachings of the Bible. The commentary on Psalm 28, published in 1531,[32] deals with the question of war against the Ottoman Turks; the commentary on Psalm 83 (1533), addresses the question of religious peace.[33] Both are subjects in which religion merges with politics.

In 1530 the German estates assembled in Augsburg to discuss matters of state. One issue confronting the Diet was the organization and financing of a campaign against the Turks, who had been repelled from Vienna with great difficulty in the preceding year. Fear of a renewed Ottoman attack on the eastern frontier of the German empire was at its height. As a councillor of Charles, Erasmus had been invited to attend the Diet, but he declined for health reasons and instead issued his advice on the question as an appendix to the psalm commentary. Erasmus's position in 1531 was remarkably similar to Luther's. The reformer, who had rejected calls for a campaign against the infidels twelve years earlier and dubbed it a papal ploy to extract money, was obliged to change course and admit the necessity of a defensive war in a treatise published in 1529.[34] Like Luther, Erasmus alluded to the dubious role played by the popes and to the general suspicion that money contributed to finance a war against the Turks ended up filling their coffers.[35] He also believed, again like Luther, that spiritual reform must precede any action against the Turks, the 'scourge of God'. He explained the lack of success of Christian armies against the Ottomans as the result of their failure to abandon 'the things which have angered God and caused him to send the Turks against us . . . they owe their victory to our sins'.[36] The first step, then, in warding off the Turks was repentance of sins. Secondly, every other expedient must be tried before waging war, and even when all possibilities were exhausted and war became inevitable, there were certain rules to be observed. The rules for just war had been laid down by St Augustine, and Erasmus merely repeated the conventional formula: 'If the war is inspired by such motives as the lust for power, ambition, private grievances, or the desire for revenge, it is clearly not a war, but mere brigandage.' Just war must be waged under legitimate authorities and ended as quickly as possible.[37] In the *Panegyricus*, a speech to welcome Philip the Fair, Erasmus had put it even more dramatically: 'It would be far better policy for the conscientious prince to maintain peace, however unjust, than start on the justest of wars.'[38] In the psalm commentary he repeated the message he had already given to princes in the *Education of a Christian Prince*: 'Although it is primarily the function of the Christian princes themselves to carry on wars, they must not resort to this most dangerous of expedients without the consent of their citizens and of the whole country.'[39] Erasmus disparaged the jingoism that fuelled so many wars, reminding his readers that they were fellow-Christians, whatever their nationality. What could be more absurd, he asked, than both sides in a war claiming to have God on their side. Did it make sense for them to pray 'Our Father, who art in Heaven, hallowed be thy name, thy will be done', at the very moment when they disregarded God's will? 'God's will is for peace', Erasmus admonished rulers, 'and you are preparing for war!'[40] And why spout nationalistic slogans to incite war? 'Reflect that this common world of ours is the fatherland to which we all belong, if the term "fatherland" has a unifying effect; that we are descended from the same forebears, if consanguinity makes men friends; that the Church is one household in which we all have an equal share, if living in the same home creates a relationship.'[41]

In considering the choice between war and peace, Erasmus also deplores the social and economic consequences of war and eloquently portrays the human misery brought on by war:

If you have ever seen towns in ruins, villages destroyed, churches burnt, and farmland abandoned and have found it a pitiable spectacle, as indeed it is, reflect that all this is the consequence of war. If you judge it a serious thing to introduce the criminal dregs of hired mercenaries into your country . . . you must realize that this is a condition of war. If you abominate robbery, this is what war teaches; if you abhor murder, this is the lesson of war . . . If neglect of the law is the most imminent threat to civil authority, why, 'the law is silent when arms prevail'. If you believe that fornication, incest and worse are loathsome evils, war is the school where these are taught. If irreverence for and neglect of religion is the source of every evil, religion is entirely swept away by the storm of war.[42]

These sentiments, expressed in the *Complaint of Peace,* are clichés but retain their emotional appeal. Not surprisingly, the work has often been reprinted and retranslated, especially during periods of crisis, from the Thirty Years' War to World War II. The fact that José Shapiro dedicated his translation of the declamation to the United Nations 'as the source of the highest hopes of our times' attests to a rather unfortunate relevance of the piece in the modern age.[43]

Given Erasmus's strong support for law and order, it is surprising to find critics in the sixteenth century accusing him of encouraging civil disobedience. These accusations were raised in connection with the Lutheran slogan of 'Christian liberty' and his use of the Bible to discount tradition. He was seen as the instigator of radical sects, like the Anabaptists, who refused to bear arms or swear an oath of allegiance to their government. Critics associated Erasmus with these manifestations of a rebellious spirit because he had used the catchphrase 'Christian liberty' and had written against warmongering princes. The accusation was, however, largely a matter of semantics. Luther's catchphrase, which referred to the deliverance of Christians from the Old Testament law, was often misinterpreted as another word for unbridled licence. The peasant rebellions of the mid-1520s and the practices of the Anabaptists were denounced by mainstream reformers, who generally stressed the need for law and order. They had no desire to alienate the princes and city councils, on whom they depended for material support. Both Luther and Erasmus were obliged to issue clarifications of their stances. Erasmus did not support liberty if it meant anarchy, and he called accusations that he was advocating defiance of secular rulers a wilful misinterpretation of his words.[44] He bitterly complained that his calls for peace were disparaged, while warmongering was condoned:

> We have made the authors of this view ['Christians must never go to war'] heretical because some pope appears to approve of war. But there is no black mark for him who disregards the teaching of Christ and his apostles and sounds the trumpet for a war, regardless of the reasons.[45]

He was prepared, however, to acknowledge the danger of unqualified pacifism. Depriving secular rulers of the right to go to war was an attack on a larger and fundamental principle: the right to punish wrongdoers. 'War in no more than judicial retribution', he wrote. In an ideal state there may be no need for retribution, but in the less than perfect society of his day it was the only method of maintaining peace and order. Biblical injunctions to refrain from retribution were counsels rather than precepts, he said. Their aim was to show us the way to perfection.[46] Yet his readers could not be entirely faulted if they read an invitation to passive resistance into the word we find in the *Complaint of Peace*:

> [The prince] should exercise his power within limits, remembering that he is a human being and a free man ruling over men who are also human and free and, finally, that he is a Christian ruler of Christians. The people in their turn should defer to him only so far as is in the public interest. A good prince should demand no more and a bad one will in fact have his desires held in check by the combined will of the citizens.[47]

CHURCH AND STATE

Erasmus's discussion of the politics of war and peace led naturally to comments on the respective roles of secular and ecclesiastical rulers in maintaining peace. The clergy, he says unequivocally, 'should intervene in wars only to put a stop to them'.[48] In one of his adages, he goes even further in limiting the role of churchmen: 'Civil dominion', he says, 'should be refused by bishops and popes'.[49] He does not shy away from naming Pope Julius II – appropriately named 'the Warrior Pope' – as an example of a man abusing his authority. Unfortunately, secular princes tend to follow the commands of the Church only when they suit their purposes, he says. 'When the pontiff calls for war, he is obeyed. If he calls for peace, why is there not the same obedience to his call?'[50]

Once again we find Erasmus's most significant statement on a political issue – the relationship between Church and state – in a devotional treatise: the *Handbook of the Christian Soldier*. This serves as an indication that this subject, like the question of law and order or of war and peace, exceeds the confines of political theory and belongs to the larger sphere of Erasmus's Christian philosophy. To begin with, Erasmus warns against reducing the thorny subject of the relationship between Church and state to simplistic terms. It is dangerous, for example, to appeal to the idea of the 'divine right of kings' and apply it to all aspects of princely rule, suggesting thereby that God endorses all aspects of a prince's rule. Rather, one must be careful to distinguish between various spheres of political activity and give them weight in proportion to their importance. The gospels provide the necessary guidelines. We may study Christ's attitude toward matters 'necessary to the ordering of a state'. There are areas, such as taxation, which he passes over in silence or treats with indifference, as if to say that he was more concerned with what was owed to God than what was owed to Caesar. Conversely, he takes a stand on the greed, vengefulness and ambition manifested by leaders, as if to say that good moral conduct was a duty they owed to God.[51]

Although Erasmus distinguishes between the duties of secular and ecclesiastical rulers, he does not draw a sharp line between their respective spheres of action. Both pursue the same goal – the welfare of the people – although their means of achieving that goal differed. Erasmus's fullest statement on the relative spheres of magistrate and clergy is embedded in his prefatory letter to the *Paraphrase on Mark* (1523):

The shepherds of the gospel have their sword, the sword of the gospel given them by Christ, with which they cut the throat of wickedness and lop off human greed. Kings have their own sword, which Christ permits them to use to strike terror into evildoers and to do honour to good men. The sword is not taken from them, but its use is delimited; they possess it for the defence of the public peace, not as safeguard for their own ambitions. There are two kinds of sword, and two kinds of kingship . . . Both priests and kings have the same end in view, though their mode of action differs, like actors playing each his own part in the same play. If each kind of kingship had its own sword always ready, that is, if they used the power entrusted to them as it should be used, we Christians (Christians in name rather than in reality) should not, I suppose, so often draw a godless sword to plunge it into the vitals of our brethren. What is more, while each kind neglects its proper duty and attempts the duty of others, neither maintains its honour or its tranquillity as it ought to do. When has a king more kingly majesty than when he sits in judgement and dispenses justice, curbs wrongdoing, settles disputes and succours the oppressed, or when he sits in council and takes thought for the prosperity of the commonwealth? When, for that matter, does a bishop enjoy more of his true dignity than when he is in the pulpit teaching the philosophy of the gospel?[52]

This description of the respective task of princes and prelates is shored up with quotations from biblical passages on the use of the sword.[53] From their interpretation it is clear that Erasmus sees the spheres of Church and state as distinct. Teaching is the task proper of the bishops; maintaining peace, justice and prosperity is the task of princes. In some comments on the subject, Erasmus emphasizes their distinct tasks; in others he emphasizes their common goal. Focusing on their tasks, he writes: 'It is *not* the [princes'] business to see that we are good, but to make us less bad and to reduce the amount of harm that bad men can do to the common weal.'[54] In another effort to set apart the respective roles of ecclesiastical and secular rulers, he suggests that princes who do not answer to their calling should be demoted to a lower rank in the hierarchical order. One might place them into the third circle together with the common people if they are no better than 'rudimentary Christians'.[55] No such suggestion is made concerning abusive and worldly ecclesiastical rulers. They are anointed priests and have received the indelible mark of the sacrament, which places them forever in the tier next to Christ. Although Erasmus makes princes liable to demotion, it does not follow that the clergy should encourage insurrection against a ruler who crosses their purpose. In the *Paraphrase on Romans* (1517), Erasmus writes: 'The state stands firm through order, it ought not to be disturbed under the pretext of religion.'[56] Thus, although the people are free by nature (according to classical tradition) and through their redemption by Christ's death (according to Christian tradition), they are still under the biblical injunction to 'give to Caesar what is Caesar's due'. While Erasmus's statements point out the distinct duties of secular and spiritual leaders, there is also an expectation that the two powers cooperate in promoting and enforcing moral goodness, which in turn will ensure stability and order. Cooperation and consensus, then, are watchwords governing social relations as well as the relationship between Church and state.

Erasmus repeats the substance of his views on Church–state relations in the *Ecclesiastes*.[57] There he speaks of a 'profane' and a 'sacred' polity, whose laws are interpreted by the *orator* (speaker in council, or diplomat) and the preacher respectively. Again he notes that the two functions are distinct but 'aiming at the same goal: the peace and tranquillity of the commonwealth'. The two powers, here represented by the diplomat and the preacher respectively, reinforce each other. Their spheres of activity coalesce in the sense that the goal of peace and tranquillity 'must be made manifest to all Christians in every action'.

Important statements on the duties and responsibilities of secular and ecclesiastical rulers can also be found in Erasmus's commentary on Psalm 83, subtitled 'On mending the Concord of the Church' (*De sarcienda ecclesiae concordia* [1533]). He interprets the division in the Church, as he interpreted the invasion of the Ottoman Turks: a scourge of God and a punishment for people's sins. 'Ungodly behaviour is the principal source of this upheaval', Erasmus states. The first step he recommended in dealing with the Turkish question was moral reform. His advice on the religious question is the same. The parties tend to blame each other, but 'we have all provoked the wrath of the Lord; it remains for all of us together to turn to him with sincere hearts'. Only then will the religious strife end. It is important for each segment of society to play its proper part. Prelates must tend to the spiritual well being of the people; princes must foster justice; the people must obey their betters. In other words, Erasmus restates in his psalm commentary what he first said about hierarchical order in the *Handbook of the Christian Soldier*. Society is divided into three classes, and each class must fulfil its assigned task. 'Let the popes . . . be the vicars of Christ, tending the Lord's flock. Let the princes administer divine justice, so that they may give an account to God in

future . . . Let lay people reverently obey their priests and loyally observe
the laws of their princes. Let each man be conscientious in his work
before Him who knows our hearts.'[58]

It is clear from the genre of the writings in which important statements
on political theory are found – the *Handbook of the Christian Soldier*, the
Paraphrase on Mark, the psalm commentaries, the handbook of preaching
– that Erasmus's political philosophy is merely an extension or an aspect
of his Christian philosophy. The works which I have cited are primarily
religious and devotional, and Erasmus tenders his advice as a member of
the clergy and writes as a homilist and exegete rather than as a political
philosopher. This was not always clear to his readers, who longed for
more practical and practicable advice. The question of collaboration
between Church and state was of great significance to the reformers in the
process of confessionalization and the accompanying differentiation
between creeds, which began in the 1530s. The process was facilitated
through the organized dissemination of religious propaganda and,
conversely, the suppression of counter-propaganda through censorship.
Indoctrination through schooling and the norming of ceremonies also
played an important role. Church ordinances were drawn up by theologians and enforced by the local secular government. In many cases, a
rigid disciplinary process led to the displacement of persons unwilling
to compromise their religious principles. Some reformers, however,
favoured the Erasmian idea of accommodation and in their ordinances
used inclusive language that permitted a certain latitude of interpretation.

The reformers active in the duchy of Jülich-Cleves tried to involve
Erasmus personally in the construction of a more tolerant state church.
The territorial ruler had for some time taken Church matters into his own
hands, as acknowledged in the current witticism that 'the Duke of Cleves
is pope in his territory'. In 1532 Duke Johann III drew up a Church order,
and his advisers, Johann von Vlatten and Konrad of Heresbach, persuaded
him to submit the ordinance to Erasmus along with a *declaratio* or interpretation of its intent. The documents, which eventually passed into a
decree, were doctrinally conservative in affirming the Real Presence and
the merit of secret confession, but were otherwise written in language
vague enough to include a wide spectrum of beliefs. The language was
too vague for Luther's taste. He immediately identified it as Erasmian in
spirit, which he equated with 'bad evangelical doctrine'. To Erasmus,
however, the document was apparently not Erasmian enough. That is to
say, it contained too much politics. He was reluctant to lend his name to
the process and to endorse the ordinance. In the poisonous atmosphere of

the religious debate, he said, his efforts to promote a spirit of accommodation might be labelled as an attempt to create yet another party, 'to
father a new sect called "moderates"'. In the next generation, the dukes of
Jülich-Cleves co-opted Joris Cassander, who was regarded as an
Erasmian. Both Cassander and his older contemporary Georg Witzel,
another admirer of Erasmus, were subsequently employed by King
Ferdinand to help with the practical settlement of the religious debate in
the Austrian lands. Erasmus's views were also mulled over in the
reformed city of Strasbourg, where Wolfgang Capito, a former confidant
of Erasmus, translated his advice 'On Mending the Concord of the
Church' into German.[59]

Whether Erasmus recognized these men as his disciples is questionable,
however. He did not answer letters from Witzel and ignored Capito, whom
he once considered his intellectual heir but disowned when he broke with
the Catholic Church.[60] He did not know Cassander, who began publishing
only in the 1530s, and who came closest to him in spirit. A comparison of
the two men's writings reveals parallels in methodology. Erasmus
habitually considered arguments on both sides of the religious question;
Cassander, too, suggested 'comparing them with equal attention and
fair judgement'. Like Erasmus, Cassander used consensus as a decision-
making tool. Searching for answers to the religious questions under
debate, he was looking for solutions that were 'distinguished by antiquity,
universality and consensus'. But although he frequently cites Erasmus,
Cassander expressly credits Vincent of Lérins with inspiring his approach
to problem-solving. This may serve as a warning against affixing the label
'Erasmian' to ideas that are likely to arise naturally out of a given set of
circumstances or have been advocated by more than one writer.[61]

5

Erasmus as biblical humanist

The edition of the New Testament published in 1516 is generally regarded as Erasmus's *opus magnum*. In modern literature, the Italian humanist Lorenzo Valla and the English divine John Colet are often depicted as his chief sources of inspiration, but the role they played in directing his course may be overrated. The movements epitomized by Valla and Colet more than the individuals themselves were shaping Erasmus's approach to biblical studies. Colet was an exponent of the Devotio Moderna, a lay movement in fifteenth-century Northern Europe which encouraged the study of Scripture as a devotional practice. Valla, a representative of Italian humanism, applied his philological skills to the gospels, comparing the standard Vulgate translation with the text in Greek manuscripts and noting discrepancies and idiomatic lapses. Both biblical humanism and the Devotio Moderna revived ideals that had been embraced and embodied in late antiquity by St Jerome. His influence on the formation of Erasmus's thought equalled, if not surpassed, that of his contemporaries. We have seen that Erasmus regarded Jerome as a principal example of learned piety, the ideal to which he himself aspired. An investigation of models that shaped Erasmus's biblical scholarship must therefore include the Church Father as well as Valla and Colet.

On his first visit to England in 1499 Erasmus made the acquaintance of John Colet, who was at that time lecturing at Oxford on the Pauline Epistles. Erasmus was drawn to the English scholar for his 'extraordinary learning and love of piety', a description reminiscent of the terms of praise Erasmus applied to Jerome.[1] Colet admonished Erasmus, a keen admirer of the classics, to devote himself to biblical rather than secular studies. He was in the habit of encouraging his students to nourish their minds 'at the choice table of the Scriptures'. Heathen books, he said, were devoid of the sweet savour of Christ. Indeed, there was nothing in them that did not savour of the devil. No Christian should partake of their fare, as he put it rather categorically, 'unless he chooses to be thought a guest of the devil rather than of the Lord'.[2] Erasmus may have focused his studies on Scripture at the urging of Colet, but he did not share his views on pagan literature or abandon his classical scholarship. Unlike his mentor, who believed that devotional fervour sufficed for an understanding of the Bible, Erasmus brought philological skills to bear on the sacred text in an effort to gain insight into its meaning. Colet was, at least initially, opposed to language studies and linguistic analysis as a means of discovering the hidden meaning of Scripture. He favoured a spiritual or meditative approach. Scripture, he wrote, 'is understood by grace; grace is procured by our prayers being heard; our prayers are heard when whetted by devotion and strengthened by fasting. To have recourse to other means is mere infatuation.'[3] Eventually, however, Erasmus persuaded him of the value of a scholarly approach to the biblical text and of the necessity of language skills, arguing that a literal understanding of the words and their historical context must precede any allegorical or spiritual interpretation. From these developments it is clear that Colet provided no more than the initial impetus for Erasmus's biblical studies.

While in England, Erasmus collected and collated Greek and Latin manuscripts of the Bible in preparation for writing a commentary on Romans. He soon came to realize, however, that his knowledge of Greek was insufficient for the task. It was imperative for him to hone his skills before he could hope to make a significant contribution to biblical studies. His financial resources were slim, but he declared heroically that he would go without a coat rather than without Greek texts, and he claimed that he undertook his journey to Italy in 1506 in order to learn Greek. Although he was exaggerating in both cases, Italy (and especially the workshop of Aldo Manuzio in Venice) offered a fertile field to pursue his interests. He found there a larger supply of texts and more opportunities to engage in discussion with kindred spirits than in Northern Europe, where Greek studies were still a novelty. By that time, Erasmus was already acquainted with Valla's critical work on the gospels undertaken in the 1450s. He discovered a manuscript of Valla's annotations when visiting the library of the Abbey of Parc near Louvain in 1504. The collation and critical notes of the Italian scholar showed him what could be achieved by taking a philological approach to the biblical text. This realization may have fired him with the ambition to undertake a similar study, but on a broader scale. The result was a bilingual, annotated edition of the New Testament. The conceptual link with Valla's work is clear from the almost identical arguments Erasmus employed in defence of the Italian scholar's annotations, which he published in 1505, and of his own New Testament edition, which appeared in 1516.

A comparison of the apologetic prefaces to the two works reveals a number of parallels. Erasmus noted that Valla braved critics who questioned his qualifications. They called it 'presumption in a grammarian . . . to let his impertinent pen loose on Holy Scripture itself'. They were shocked that he dared to write annotations 'after comparing several old and good Greek manuscripts'. After all, it is from Greek sources that our text undoubtedly comes, and 'Valla's notes had to do with internal disagreements, or a nodding translator's plainly inadequate renderings of the meaning, or things that are more intelligibly expressed in Greek, or, finally anything that is clearly corrupt in our texts'.[4] The theologians were wrong to accuse Valla of trespassing on their territory:

This whole business of translating the Holy Scriptures is manifestly a grammarian's function . . . I do not really believe that Theology herself, the queen of all the sciences, will be offended if some share is claimed in her and due deference shown to her by her humble attendant Grammar; for, though Grammar is of less consequence in some men's eyes, no help is more indispensable than hers . . . Perhaps she discusses trivial questions, but these have important corollaries.

Theologians insisted that the interpretation of the Bible depended on divine inspiration, but Jerome had pointed out the role scholarship played: 'Scholarship, together with the resources of language, conveys the meaning it apprehends.' Erasmus concluded that 'those who venture to write, not merely on the Scriptures, but on any ancient books at all, are devoid of both intelligence and modesty if they do not possess a reasonable command of both Greek and Latin'.[5]

In the prolegomena to his own New Testament, Erasmus repeated these arguments in favour of applying philological skills to the scriptural text. Theologians were wrong to require inspiration from anyone who examined the text, he said, once again quoting Jerome's distinction between the prophet and the translator.[6] In his dedicatory letter to Pope Leo X, Erasmus described his work as he had earlier on described Valla's: 'I correct [the text] where it is corrupt, in some places I explain its obscurities, and this I do . . . on the evidence of very ancient copies.'[7] In a letter to the Reader, he defended the use of philology ('grammar') in terms similar to those used in the preface to Valla's notes: Points of grammar may be minute, but 'because of these minute points we see even the greatest theologians sometimes make discreditable mistakes'. The philologist deals with the letter of the text, but 'on it rests the mystic meaning'.[8] The scriptural text was in need of revision because it had been corrupted by 'the carelessness or ignorance of scribes' and by a translator 'who nodded or was under a delusion'.[9] The parallels between the apologetic preface to Valla's annotations and the prolegomena to Erasmus's New Testament edition a decade later amount to an acknowledgement of their common aims and suggest that the discovery of Valla's work had considerable impact on Erasmus's own scholarly ambitions. At the same time, we must remember that he was already firmly launched on his course when he came upon the manuscript of Valla's annotations and that the discovery was in fact a by-product of his search for source material.

When the New Testament edition was at the planning stage, critics attempted to discourage Erasmus from the undertaking, arguing that he had, first of all, been anticipated by Valla and more recently by Jacques Lefèvre and, secondly, that he would face the same objections they had encountered. Erasmus refused to be frightened off by the prospect of unpopularity or controversy.[10] He was convinced that his approach was well founded and would eventually carry the day. He furthermore rejected the notion that he was following in Lefèvre's footsteps, pointing out that he had only lately become aware of the French scholar's parallel attempts to annotate the Bible. Neither Valla's nor Lefèvre's work, moreover, was coextensive with his own, he noted. They provided critical notes rather than a critical text: a process that did not require editorial decisions. Valla's notes were, moreover, confined to the gospels and, as he himself attested, based on the slim evidence of seven manuscripts. Erasmus's annotations covered the whole of the New Testament and were based on a dozen manuscripts. He continued his search for manuscripts after the text and annotations were published and incorporated his findings in later editions. Moreover, he surveyed and carefully recorded the variants found in patristic citations of biblical passages.

Erasmus answered the principal objections to his undertaking in a polemical exchange with the Louvain theologian Maarten van Dorp. Dorp's open letter, published in 1514, represented the views of his colleagues on the faculty of theology. Erasmus rebutted the arguments proffered in Dorp's letter, alleging that the assumptions underlying his criticism were wrong. Dorp and his colleagues did not understand the process of textual transmission and the inherent danger of corruption. The

Vulgate, of which they were so protective, was not sacrosanct. Contrary to a widely held belief, it was not the work of St Jerome, written under divine guidance and authorized by Pope Damasus. Jerome merely corrected mistakes that marred the texts circulating in his time. There was no record that Jerome's version was formally authorized, either in his own time or through the decision of a later council. Nor could it be denied that the *textus receptus* had once again been corrupted by scribes and stood in need of another revision. Erasmus stressed, moreover, that editing the text did not constitute a challenge to the authority of the Church. His edition was meant for scholars and not intended to replace the text used in churches and universities.

It was ironical that biblical humanists like Erasmus faced the same arguments as Jerome in his time, as Thomas More noted when he came to the defence of his friend. 'Every single objection you make', he told Dorp, 'was once made against St Jerome and thoroughly refuted by him.'[11] Indeed, some of the expressions used by Erasmus to defend himself and Valla are taken word for word from Jerome's apologetic prefaces to individual biblical books. Among the quotations is the derisive reference to people who are adverse to change and cling to the popular wisdom that 'old wine is better'; the distinction between the prophet writing under divine inspiration and the translator relying on language skills;[12] and the complaint that the scriptural text was corrupted by inattentive scribes and ignorant translators.[13] The echoes show that Erasmus was consciously following in Jerome's footsteps. He was, moreover, a contributor to an edition of Jerome's *Opera omnia*, which appeared in the same year (1516) and from the same press (Johann Froben in Basel) as his own critical New Testament edition. The preface, which Erasmus supplied to the works of Jerome, confirms the Church Father's influence on his own scholarship. He called Jerome 'chief among the theologians of the Latin world, and in fact almost the only writer we have who deserves the name of theologian'. The description of Jerome's accomplishments which follows reads like a list of prerequisites for a biblical humanist. He was 'eloquent, a master of the tongues, [had] a range of knowledge in all antiquity and all history . . . and a perfect command of Holy Scripture'.[14]

Erasmus, like Jerome, directed his arguments first of all against the resistance to change that springs from mental sloth and secondly against pious but uneducated people who feared contamination of the sacred text with pagan style. *Elegantia*, or purity of language, was unimportant to these readers. God's truth needed no embellishment, they argued.

In Erasmus's time, new objections were added to the old complaints faced by Jerome. One issue that came to the fore was the question of academic qualifications needed to deal with the sacred text. The theologians at the universities regarded humanists as rank amateurs trespassing on their professional territory. They were merely 'grammarians' and likely to introduce heterodox thought on account of their ignorance of the subject matter. On a practical level, theologians feared that new editions would wreak havoc on classroom practices and spoil carefully constructed proofs based on the wording of the Vulgate texts. Greek and Hebrew were not part of the curriculum taught to theology students. The idea that a theologian should be able to consult the original text posed a challenge to the older university professors and endangered their carefully cultivated image of authority. Many of these objections had first been brought against fifteenth-century humanists such as Valla and were still current in the sixteenth century when Erasmus prepared his edition of the New Testament. Lectureships in Hebrew and Greek had now been established at some universities in the North, but this merely aggravated the issue, as students flocked to the new lecturers and deserted the teachers of traditional subjects. The competition between theologians and humanists was no longer just a matter of competence but also of remuneration. The newly endowed chairs sometimes carried a higher stipend than was offered to lecturers who were graduates of the traditional, scholastic system. The flight of students to the humanists meant financial losses for the old-style professors, who derived a part of their pay from attendance and examination fees. Thus professional envy, fear of heterodoxy and resistance to change combined to create an adversarial climate for humanists at Northern universities.

It had been Erasmus's original plan to publish the Greek text of the New Testament and to furnish it with explanatory notes. On the urging of his publisher, he juxtaposed the Greek text with a slightly emended Latin Vulgate. The notes justified the editorial changes, pointed out discrepancies between the Greek and the Latin text, and errors or idiomatic lapses in the Latin. In many cases, too, Erasmus elucidated the meaning of a word or phrase by reference to classical usage. On the whole, the annotations accompanying the first edition of the New Testament (1516) were the work of a classical philologist, to use a modern designation. The Greek text was the first edition to reach the market. While Erasmus was preparing his text, another polyglot edition was going forward in Alcala under the direction of Cardinal Jimenes de Cisneros. Its printing was completed in 1514, but the long wait for the papal imprimatur delayed its distribution until 1522. The Erasmian New Testament was therefore *de facto* the *editio princeps*.

Critical reaction to the edition resulted in revisions to the text and a corresponding increase in notes. The changes introduced in the editions of 1519, 1522, 1527 and 1535 altered the character of the apparatus. While the original notes had been largely explanatory, the added material had an apologetic thrust. Furthermore, the need to respond to critics who discussed the doctrinal import of Erasmus's editorial changes shifted the emphasis from philological to theological issues. Even in the first edition Erasmus had been careful to justify his enterprise in the prolegomena. He tried to anticipate objections and disarm his critics with well-aimed arguments. In the original edition, the prolegomena included a dedicatory letter to Pope Leo X and a letter to the Reader. In addition they contained a formal *Apologia*, the *Methodus* (later published in an expanded version under the title *Ratio*), in which Erasmus emphasized the need for language studies in the formation of theologians,[15] and the *Paraclesis*, a homiletic piece on the inherent power of the divine Word to change and save those who listened to God's message. In the second edition, Erasmus added to the prolegomena a tract entitled *Against his Morose and Captious Critics*, in which he linked his work expressly with Jerome's textual criticism. The piece concluded with a long list of distinguished supporters who endorsed his work. He furthermore included the pope's gracious reply to his dedicatory letter. Although this did not amount to a papal imprimatur, Erasmus clearly hoped to impress his readers and convince them of the wide acceptance his work had found among the leaders of the Church. Humanistic friends congratulated him on his success, and the edition sold briskly, but it continued to be unpopular with scholastic theologians, who remained unimpressed by the prolegomena. The Paris doctor Pierre Cousturier scoffed at the pope's letter of endorsement. It signified nothing, he wrote, since Leo X was no theologian.[16] Nothing would do but the official imprimatur, which was not a polite gesture but the outcome of a close scrutiny by a committee of professional theologians.

While principal objections to textual criticism declined over time, objections to specific passages in Erasmus's edition multiplied. University theologians undertook detailed reviews of his textual changes and the annotations justifying them, and accused him of heterodox statements on a number of issues, ranging from the divine nature of Christ to the institution of the sacrament of penance and the origin of adult baptism. Polemical tracts against Erasmus's edition began to appear in 1518, starting with the dialogue by the Louvain theologian Jacques Masson, who questioned the need for language studies and insisted that the scholastic approach provided safe answers to all doctrinal questions.[17] Between 1520 and 1529 a slew of theologians wrote against Erasmus, among them Edward Lee, later archbishop of York, Diego López de Zúñiga, a contributor to the Complutensian Polyglot, Alberto Pio, a learned diplomat at the papal court, and Frans Titelmans, a disciple of Masson and fellow member of the Louvain faculty of theology. They accused Erasmus of shoddy workmanship, doctrinal misinterpretations, blasphemy and impiety, but stopped short of calling him a heretic. More dangerous than the attacks of these individuals were the corporate investigations of the Spanish Inquisition and of the faculty of theology of Paris. The latter in particular had behind it the full weight of tradition and enjoyed an international prestige that made its pronouncements authoritative in the Christian world.

In 1527 Alonso Manrique, the Inquisitor-General, called a meeting at Valladolid to discuss suspect passages in Erasmus's works. Two weeks later the conference was suspended because of an outbreak of the plague. It was never reconvened. Manrique's willingness to allow the inquisitorial process to lapse attests to Erasmus's popularity and standing at the Spanish court. Charles V, German emperor and King of Spain, himself wrote to Erasmus, assuring him that he had nothing to fear from an investigation. 'There is no risk in my having permitted an inquisition into your books', he announced confidently. 'If any human error is found in them you yourself may, on being admonished in civil fashion, correct or explain it such that it will no longer give offence to the weak, and in this manner you will make your work immortal and stop the mouths of your detractors. If, however, nothing is found that deserves criticism, you can see how much glory you will win for yourself and your works.'[18] In fact, there is every indication that the investigation was carefully orchestrated and directed from above to ensure that Erasmus's reputation should not be damaged. Pope Clement VII, from whom the Inquisitor-General received his instructions, declared that he was 'grieved' at hearing that Erasmus's writings had come under suspicion. After all, Erasmus was a man 'famous for his learning and eloquence, who had written much that was highly praised, and who deserved praise for rebuking Luther.' He asked Manrique to investigate and determine whether any writings of Erasmus needed to be expurgated. In the meantime, he said, attacks on the Dutch scholar must stop. In future, he declared, 'no preachers should speak of Erasmus in other than terms of respect'.[19] Manrique in turn instructed the examiners to submit their reports to him, reminding them at the same time that 'the decision whether there was anything wrong or dangerous in Erasmus's works did not lie with them'.[20] In the event, records of discussions carried on at the short-lived Valladolid conference show that the arbiters were by no means united in their judgement of Erasmus. Some did indeed accuse him of unorthodox remarks on the nature of the Trinity, on the divinity of Christ and on the sacrament of penance. Others, however, conceded that his thought was orthodox, but noted his failure to use the 'proper' (i.e. scholastic) terminology. His friends regarded the outcome of the investigation, or rather its termination, as a victory for him. 'It has been made clear to everyone that your enemies were motivated by envy. They have fought in vain and paid their dues, overpowered by the witness Truth', one of his Spanish correspondents wrote. The reports of the examiners were soon leaked to the public, however, and Erasmus's own, more sober reaction was: 'I would rather suffer defeat than win this sort of victory.'[21] While Spanish attempts to inveigle Erasmus fizzled, a contemporary investigation at the University of Paris took its course and eventually ended in a formal condemnation of certain passages in his writings.

The investigation was at first the personal quest of Noël Béda, the syndic (or chair) of the faculty and focused, not on the New Testament, but on Erasmus's *Paraphrases on the New Testament*. Homiletic in tone, they formed a continuous commentary on the gospels and epistles. Although on the whole well received, the *Paraphrases* gave offence to some readers because Erasmus put the narrative into the apostle's and occasionally Christ's mouth, (i.e. he hid his own interpretation of the text under the persona of the evangelist or the Son of God). In 1526 the Paris printer Konrad Resch requested permission from the *parlement* of Paris to reprint the *Paraphrase on Luke*. Following standard procedure, the *parlement* sought the advice of the faculty of theology. Béda as the faculty's deputy read the work and detected many 'Lutheranisms'. Accordingly, Resch was refused permission to publish the book.

For some years, Erasmus had enjoyed immunity from official criticism in France, protected by the goodwill of King Francis I, who admired the humanist and personally invited him to join the nascent Collège de France. Under the influence of his sister, the reform-minded Marguerite of Navarre, the king extended his protection also to other writers whose orthodoxy was questioned by the Paris theologians. The faculty chafed at the bit but could not act against the royal command. In 1526, however, Francis lost the battle of Pavia against the imperial troops and became a prisoner of Charles V in Spain. During his year-long absence from France, the theologians were free to promote their own agenda. In these circumstances, Erasmus found it politic to initiate a correspondence with Béda, either to pacify him or to stall an investigation into his works which was now in the offing. The correspondence, which began civilly enough, soon took on an acid tone and ended with Béda publishing his critique of Erasmus's *Paraphrase*. On the syndic's initiative, the faculty of theology then undertook a broader investigation of Erasmus's writings, which resulted in a formal censure. Erasmus protested against Béda's actions in tracts addressed to the faculty and the *parlement*, but in vain. The faculty's censures were published in 1531.

Aware of the support Erasmus enjoyed in high places, the theologians were cautious in wording their judgement. They avoided declaring Erasmus a heretic, although they linked him with Luther. The purpose of their censures, they wrote, was to 'fend off the dangers inherent in suspect books or in those that are not free of the poison of the condemned doctrines of Wycliff and Luther'.[22] First and foremost, the verdict militated against what Béda had called 'theologizing humanists'. The faculty issued a stern warning to those who foolishly regarded 'whatever was clothed in splendid speech as true and, by contrast, whatever was expressed in plain and unpolished speech as false'. This struck at Erasmus's efforts to correct the grammar of the Vulgate translator and to reword awkward phrases in the classical idiom. The faculty further warned biblical humanists that 'knowing Greek and Hebrew [did not] mean being a perfect and consummate theologian, for men who know only that and have not otherwise been instructed in the discipline of theology are to be considered grammarians, not theologians'.[23] The faculty's verdict gave voice to the desire of the theologians for a 'closed shop' approach to biblical studies. They insisted that editing, translating or interpreting Scripture could not be undertaken without proper academic qualifications. While humanists generally accepted the exclusive right of theologians to exegesis and doctrinal pronouncements, they (somewhat disingenuously) suggested that editing and translating were purely philological tasks. In the prolegomena to his New Testament, Erasmus had declared that he was concerned only with textual criticism and left exegesis to professional theologians. In making this claim, he boldly ignored the fact that words and meaning could not be separated and that translation was a form of interpretation.

The judgement of the Paris faculty had been preceded by individual attacks on Erasmus by Paris graduates: for example Pierre Cousturier, whose criticism has already been cited, and Josse Clichtove, who had for a while shown a progressive spirit and even a certain animus against his more traditional colleagues, but who in the end was cowed into submission. By writing against Erasmus he presumably proved his loyalty to the Parisians, as Dorp had done before him in testimony to his allegiance to the Louvain theologians. In fact, Erasmus quipped, writing against him seemed to have become a prerequisite of obtaining a doctorate in theology.[24]

While the reaction of theologians to Erasmus was expressly hostile in France, Spain and in the German empire, and written attacks on Erasmus were echoed by conservative professors in their lectures and by preachers in the pulpit, the situation in Italy was more complex. The papal court was determined to avoid a confrontation with a man of Erasmus's scholarly stature and wide-ranging influence. Leo X had officially welcomed his work on the New Testament. His successors suppressed the anti-Erasmian tracts of López de Zúñiga, who was obliged to publish them furtively in the interims following Leo's and Adrian VI's death. Adrian himself had refused to act on a request of the University of Louvain, whose chancellor he was, to initiate an investigation into Erasmus's writings. His successor, Clement VII, expressly cautioned critics against provoking Erasmus, as the papal legate Girolamo Aleandro attested. 'It is well known', he wrote, 'that the Holy Apostolic See would long ago have condemned many of his opinions, if they had not been afraid to provoke him to worse action'. The Spaniard Juan Ginés Sepúlveda, another man intimately familiar with the policies of the papal court, confirmed the strategy. Clement VII, he wrote, wanted criticism of Erasmus suppressed out of fear that he would join the reformers' camp. 'During his lifetime the popes kept up good relations with him', he wrote, 'not because they approved his writings and doctrines, but to avoid exasperating him. They wished to prevent him from publicly parting with the Catholic Church and openly crossing over to the Lutheran camp, for in this manner he would destroy the counsels of the Church.' He added that this was not his own interpretation, but 'was indicated to me personally by Clement VII'.[25] Criticism that did reach the public was muted. The Italian theologians Lanzelotto de' Politi and Agostino Steuco, for example, wrote against Erasmus but disguised the target of their criticism and did not name him. A third critic, the papal notary Alberto Pio, published his review of Erasmus's writings only after he had gone to live in France and was encouraged and perhaps aided there by Béda. Girolamo Aleandro, who served in Germany during the crucial years of the Diet of Worms and suspected Erasmus's loyalty, as we have seen, kept his criticism confidential and confined letters voicing his suspicions to the diplomatic pouch.

Erasmus's response to published criticism was defiant, although it must be said that defiance was his last stand. His preferred tactic and first line of defence was to explain away all criticisms as misunderstandings. He tried moreover to forestall criticism by carefully hedging his statements. We shall see that his ambivalence had in fact a legitimate epistemological basis, but his critics saw in it merely a strategy of concealment. Alberto Pio challenged Erasmus angrily to state his views unequivocally and make sure that his meaning was 'not veiled, not convoluted, not ambiguous, not slippery, but clear'.[26] Erasmus hoped that circumlocution would keep his critics at bay, but when this tactic failed, he became truculent. Against the advice of his friends, he matched every published attack with a pugnacious response of his own. He explained that this was necessary because readers took the accusations of his critics at face value and did not go to the trouble of verifying them or assessing their merits by reading the censured passages. He himself was therefore obliged to supply readers with the counter-arguments. Secondly, while criticism of his scholarship could have been overlooked, the implication that his writings were blasphemous, impious or even heterodox could not be passed over. 'It is impious to put up with the slanderous accusation of impiety', he wrote.[27] In fact, however, Erasmus answered both types of accusations – shoddy workmanship and heterodoxy – with the same zeal, tenacity and air of contempt. Contemporaries took note of his combative spirit. Agostino Steuco, for one, complained: 'You flare up and rush into polemics if anyone as much as touches you.'[28] When the Louvain theologian Eustachius Sichem wrote against him, he fully expected Erasmus to 'maintain his positions, as usual, with a new apologia'.[29] He was no doubt greatly surprised to find that his attack was one of the very few Erasmus ignored. The restraint Erasmus showed in that case was, however, governed by external circumstances. He had lodged a complaint against the Louvain theologians at the papal and the imperial courts. As a consequence, silence was imposed on both parties, and Erasmus had to shelve polemics he had at hand.[30]

Although the predominant mood in Erasmus's apologiae is denial and defiance, he employs a range of strategies to rationalize his rejection of criticism. We can identify three stratagems, or escape routes, which Erasmus employed routinely. He claimed that the remarks singled out for criticism were not definite pronouncements but suggestions; that they were not his own opinions but citations from another man's work; or that they were concerned with grammatical usage, not meaning. Examples of the first type of disclaimer – that he was not offering judgement, but merely food for thought and leaving the final verdict to others – are numerous in his annotations on the New Testament and in his *apologiae*. He was engaging in arguments 'out of intellectual curiosity' and to explore options, he said. He was making 'a modest proposal' and leaving the matter in the hands of his readers, or of professional theologians, or of those who had teaching authority. Nowhere did he 'anticipate the judgement of scholars', he wrote in the prolegomena to the New Testament. He spoke 'without prejudice to the authority of the universities. Everyone is free to pass his own judgement. I am writing notes, not passing laws; I propose matter for discussion, not for immediate adoption.'[31]

The second strategy is most often used in defence of outspoken comments in works of fiction such as the *Colloquies* or the *Praise of Folly*. If the views expressed there were attacked, Erasmus routinely took cover behind the persona of the speaker or of the genre itself. The *Folly* was a satire, he pointed out. 'Whoever heard of a humorous subject being submitted for rigorous examination to theologians?'[32] In the *Colloquies*, too, he had spoken *per lusum*, in jest. The opinions expressed were those of the speaker in question and were of course tailored to suit the *dramatis persona*. To be credible, a 'fool' said silly things, a 'criminal' performed evil deeds, and a 'reformer' was given lines that challenged the status quo. The character in a piece of fiction did not express the beliefs of the author. 'But if I introduced a Turk as speaker', Erasmus said sarcastically, 'they would no doubt attribute to me whatever he says.'[33] Similarly the Paris theologians examined his *Paraphrases* as if 'the words spoken by a third person were mine'. His censors did not take into account the dramatic voice. 'By that reasoning anything said by impious men in the text could be attributed to me, and I shall unite in my person Christ, Paul and Caiphas. One cannot write paraphrases without taking into consideration the dramatis persona.'[34]

In defending his annotations on the New Testament, Erasmus often used the third strategy: claiming that he was merely concerned with correct usage. He insisted on narrowly circumscribing his task as textual criticism. 'I played the role of a grammarian', he said,[35] blissfully ignoring the fact that the verbal changes he made affected the meaning of the passage. The example most often cited by his critics was the change from *poenitentiam agite* (do penance) to *poeniteat vos* (repent) at Matt. 1:3, which seemed to diminish the importance of the traditional penance imposed by the father confessor and support Luther's attack on the priest's mediating role. Another notorious example was the translation of Greek *mysterion*, often rendered in the Vulgate by *sacramentum*. The word s*acramentum* (literally, something holy) could have the technical meaning 'sacrament'. In some cases, Erasmus replaced *sacramentum* with *mysterium* (something holy and ineffable), a word that lacked the technical dimension. The change had obvious doctrinal implications. One Spanish critic, Sancho Carranza, suggested that Erasmus's translation inspired Luther to deny the sacramental character of matrimony and of penance.[36] Similarly, Carranza protested Erasmus's observation that Christ was rarely called 'God' in the gospels. Erasmus had written: 'I don't know whether there is any passage in the letters of the apostles or evangelists where the epithet "God" is clearly given to Christ, except in one or two places.' Defending his observation, Erasmus explained that he was discussing biblical usage and had no intention of questioning the divinity of Christ.[37] The modifications and explanations, which Erasmus offered in later editions of the New Testament were a tacit acknowledgement of the doctrinal implications of his editorial changes, even if he was unwilling to concede that point openly.

Although there is a great deal of subterfuge in Erasmus's apologiae, they are not devoid of substantive arguments. In many cases he was no doubt right to repudiate his critics. Some of their objections were rooted in ideology; others betrayed ignorance. In such cases Erasmus carefully built up his argument by aligning himself with irrefutable authorities. He quoted Jerome and Augustine in support of his views and challenged his critics to argue against them. Since he was dealing with scholastically trained theologians, he gleefully cited their own authorities to counter their arguments: 'If it is unlawful to investigate the rational behind papal decrees [as some critics had alleged], they must condemn Thomas, Scotus, Durandus, and innumerable other [scholastic] theologians.'[38] When Béda suggested that Erasmus was lacking in scholastic training and counselled him to read, among others, Jean Gerson, Erasmus pointed out with great satisfaction that he was following Gerson in deprecating the quibbling disputations of the scholastics. Erasmus furthermore recognized that attack was the best defence, and questioned the qualifications, procedures and motives of his critics in turn. He had good reason to quarrel with the careless (or deliberately vague) references of his critics. They quoted him inaccurately, he protested, or out of context; they wove a patchwork from disconnected passages and left out important qualifiers.

He used this argument in defending himself against the verdict of the Paris theologians. They had not followed proper procedure, he alleged. They were basing their verdict on excerpts gathered by a group of over-zealous deputies. He even suggested that the verdict lacked the endorsement of the majority and therefore had no validity. One is reminded of Luther's famous objection to the pope's condemnation of his works as impious or heretical, 'respectively'. Luther challenged the authorities to be specific and name the works and point out the passages that were heretical. Similarly Erasmus objected to having passages culled from his works and censored wholesale. 'It is the first duty of a legitimate inquisitor to quote verbatim the words that, in his opinion, contain some impiety, then to add briefly what it is in these words that gives offence', he lectured his critics.[39] Béda's critique, for example, consisted of a long list of passages, followed in each case by the laconic verdict 'Lutheran'. It was not fair, Erasmus complained, to use incriminating labels without giving reasons for doing so. The theologians disdained Erasmus's work because he had no academic training, but he in turn found it galling to be obliged to deal with men 'who had become theologians without the benefit of philology', who 'know neither Greek nor Latin and cavil at what they don't understand'.[40]

In spite of Erasmus's protestations that he would not descend to trading insults, he had no qualms calling his censors' criticism 'drivel and slander' and the authors 'stupid, ignorant, boorish and malicious'.[41] There was in his apologiae a healthy dose of arrogance and aggressiveness. Although he addressed the faculties of theology at Paris and Louvain respectfully, he hit individual critics very hard, calling them incompetent or malicious and accusing them of acting from personal ambition rather than scholarly motives. For that reason, he declared, he owed them no gratitude, even when they pointed out factual mistakes. He made the requested changes grudgingly and kept them to a minimum. He did publish a list entitled *Passages in Some of Erasmus's Works which Have been Revised by Himself* (*Loca quaedam in aliquot Erasmi lucubrationibus per ipsum emendata*, 1529), but the title raised expectations that remained unfulfilled. The list consisted mostly of corrections of typographical errors and other minor slips. One senses that Erasmus regarded even that small gesture a great sacrifice. He was anxious to explain that he was making no concessions to his critics. It was human to err, but 'nowhere shall I admit the charge of impiety'. Nor was this an effort to appease the enemy. 'Someone will perhaps expect me to change everything ever criticized by anyone. But that would be corruption, not correction.'[42] Erasmus's reaction to criticism strikes the modern reader as ungracious and aroused comment also in his own time when scholarly exchanges were sharper than they are now. Even an admirer like Ambrosius Pelargus felt that Erasmus's responses lacked sincerity. 'I fear', he told him, 'that there will be no shortage of people who will regard your words as a smokescreen.'[43]

Erasmus, however, insisted that he had done the right thing. In a letter to Jacobo Sadoleto, who urged him to refrain from further polemics, he defended himself vigorously. People accused him wrongly of being pugnacious. 'I have written numerous apologiae', he said, 'but no invectives'. He had in fact ignored many attacks and 'in those I answered, I surpassed [my critics] in modesty and civility'. He had always been a reluctant polemicist. 'For a long time I restrained myself', he wrote, 'even though I was harassed frequently and in an odious manner, but when they proceeded to cast aspersions on my piety, I could no longer keep silent, nor was it right to keep silent.' He was especially bitter that what he had written before Luther came on the stage was interpreted retroactively as 'Lutheran'. He wished that he 'could start everything over again', but times were such that it was as dangerous to speak out as it was to keep silent.[44]

So far I have dealt with serious allegations and equally serious responses, but not all of Erasmus's battles were fought in the halls of academe or before an inquisitorial board. Erasmus's humanistic friends fought back on his behalf with their favourite strategic tool: satire. Occasionally Erasmus himself made use of that weapon. Dorp, Masson, Lee and Nicolaus Baechem, who preached against Erasmus in Louvain, all made their appearance in lampoons. In 1518, shortly after visiting Erasmus in Louvain, Wilhelm Nesen wrote a comic skit featuring the faculty of theology. Erasmus had certainly inspired the piece, if not actually collaborated with his friend. In the skit the Louvain professors march in a funeral procession, taking the Muse to her final resting place. Dorp appears under the name of 'Phenacus' (Trickster). Masson is said to walk with a limp, the consequence of courting a married woman. The writer explains that Masson had been obliged to jump from a window in a bid to escape the irate husband. Lee makes an appearance as 'Phthonides', son of Malice. He is described as a pale, skinny fellow who walks with a mincing step and 'grins sardonically'.[45] Nesen is also the supposed author of another satire on 'S. Nicolaus', that is Nicolaus Baechem. The 'S' did not stand for 'Saint' but for 'Stupid', as readers discovered on delving into the text. Erasmus himself routinely referred to

Baechem, who was a member of the Carmelite Order, as 'the camelite'. In the *Colloquies* a character recounts that he 'heard a "camel" preach that everything new was to be shunned'. In that case, his friend jokes, the man 'deserved never to change his old shoes or dirty underwear, always to eat rotten eggs, and drink nothing but mouldy wine'.[46] Lee makes an appearance in another humanistic lampoon, *Hochstratus ovans*, attributed to Ulrich von Hutten. He is cast as a pig born in a Carmelite pen, which dies and is reincarnated as a long-tailed dog. 'Long-tailed', an ethnic slur on the English, appears also in one of Erasmus's colloquies. The 'long-tailed Scotist' with the perpetual grin was not difficult to identify since Lee had been described in the similar terms in Nesen's skit. In an anonymous satire entitled *Decoctio*, Lee is diagnosed as mad. He is submerged in a herbal bath, which cures him of his sickness and allows him to appreciate scholars like Erasmus. Lee makes another appearance, together with Dorp, in the skit *The Council of Theologists*, attributed to Crotus Rubeanus. In that skit Dorp is named 'Professor Duplicius'. Lee, who speaks in his own name, confesses that he has taken up Greek only to criticize Erasmus. Béda appears as a character in Erasmus's colloquy 'A Meeting of the Philological Society', in which the meaning of 'Natalis' (the Latin form of Noël) is discussed and the suggestion made that it is a derivative of 'nates': buttocks. The name of another critic, Pierre Cousturier (in Latin, Petrus Sutor), is derived from 'sutorium': shoe black.[47]

The lampoons reinforce our impression that Erasmus was in no mood to suffer his critics gladly. In the 1520s, however, he himself became the target of satire, as both Catholics and Protestants resented his reluctance to choose sides. He was derided as 'Errasmus' (Prone to error), Proteus (the mythical figure who can change shape at will) and in one particularly crude satire made the victim of grave robbery. In the *Funeral of Erasmus*, his body is torn to pieces and flung into the sewer by an angry crowd of monks.[48] It was clear that Erasmus had passed the zenith of his career, as he himself acknowledged in 1524: 'My popularity, if I had any, has either cooled off so far that it scarcely exists, or has quite evaporated, or even has turned into hatred.'[49] He had the misfortune of living in times when radicalism was counted as a virtue and compromise was equalled with hypocrisy and moral cowardice. It was the age of confessionalization, the entrenchment of confessional differences, and the *Mittelhauf* (the motley middle), as Melanchthon disdainfully called the moderates, were not appreciated by either Catholics or reformers.

6

Why Erasmus was no Lutheran: Christian scepticism and the importance of consensus

Erasmus's early criticism of Church abuses led to expectations that he would throw his support behind the reformers. Instead he chose to 'be a spectator rather than an actor'[1] and staunchly refused to become the champion of any religious party. As the confessional strife escalated, however, he found it increasingly difficult to maintain a pose of detachment. He was a prominent writer and inextricably linked with the religious question by his clerical status. His calls for reform were on record. Both Lutherans and Catholics who favoured reform from within were looking to Erasmus for leadership. In fact it is striking how many people depicted their confessional choice as one between Erasmus and Luther. They did not use Erasmus as shorthand for 'Catholic' and Luther for 'schismatic'. Rather, they regarded them as representative of two approaches to the religious question. Melanchthon hinted at the difference when he said that Luther was a true preacher of the gospel, whereas Erasmus merely taught civility. This implied that Luther was concerned with substance, Erasmus with form; that Luther was principled, Erasmus non-committal. Depending on their leanings, contemporaries used sharper language to characterize the respective approaches of the two men. Critics of Luther thought him recalcitrant rather than principled, rebellious rather than heroic; critics of Erasmus regarded him as hypocritical rather than diplomatic, cowardly rather than irenic. Sylvius Egranus, for example, was willing to grant Luther

a good mind and acumen, but judgement, erudition and prudence I find completely lacking in him, while I see these qualities abundantly present in Erasmus. I therefore like Erasmus's meek spirit, or as they call it, his 'fear' better than Luther's boldness, his insulting and aggressive manner, his ardour and vehemence, which has had no other effect so far than to mingle heaven and earth and turn everything upside down.[2]

Johannes Cochlaeus was another man who preferred Erasmus's approach. Luther, he said, was troublesome and pugnacious. 'Erasmus acts more prudently and produces more useful results with less upheaval and unpopularity.'[3] Personal friends of the two men found it painful to make a decision that would turn one of them into an enemy. Udalricus Zasius, for example, promised 'not to desert [Erasmus], the most learned man in the whole world, that is, I won't desert him but I wish no evil to Luther, a man of exceptional learning and of more than exemplary consistency'. Boniface Amerbach likewise confessed that he was in a quandary whom to follow. Zwingli was similarly uneasy in 1521: 'In each man there is something that can be most helpful to us and in no way harmful . . . yet each man has his peculiar qualities (no offence meant). If one of them combined both qualities, he would be incomparably superior to the other.' Zwingli does not specify what those qualities are. Presumably he alludes to Luther's steadfastness, which verged on intransigence, and to Erasmus's diplomacy, which could easily translate into fence-sitting. 'Why, then, do not both serve us, each in his capacity?' he lamented.[4]

Erasmus offers a number of explanations as to why he preferred to remain on the sidelines of the debate, some of them rather mundane. Outspoken partisans were bound to suffer persecution, he said. He did not want to run the risk of becoming an exile: 'Age and health do not permit me to wander about or live in poverty or to hide somewhere and flee from place to place.' He was no hero, or rather, he was willing to be a martyr for Christ, but not for Luther. He wanted reform, yes, but he respected authority and wished to go through the right channels. People accused him of 'being too fond of peace. But, to speak frankly, I would rather err on that side, not so much because it is safer, but also because it is more pious.'[5] The fundamental concept, however, that informed Erasmus's irenicism and his reluctance to champion any one party, was epistemological. When a public showdown became unavoidable, the work he wrote against Luther clearly demonstrated that his approach to the religious question was predicated on what I shall call 'Christian scepticism'.

The changing dynamics of the relationship between Luther and Erasmus are evident from their correspondence in the years 1519–24. It was Luther who first approached Erasmus in 1519 with a letter full of conventional fawning. 'For who is there in whose heart Erasmus does not occupy a central place, to whom Erasmus is not the teacher who holds him in thrall?' he wrote.[6] A model of humanistic networking, Luther's letter included a ritual sideswiping of scholastic writers and an invocation of the names of mutual friends to establish common ground.[7] The letter was a plea for friendship, couched in the usual clichés of self-abasement: 'And so, dear Erasmus, kindest of men, if you see no objection, accept this younger brother of yours in Christ, who is at least much devoted to you and full of affection, though in his ignorance he has deserved nothing better than to bury himself in a corner.'[8] Luther, then, was uncharacteristically meek in this first approach to his famous contemporary.[9] Erasmus's reply is benevolent but somewhat condescending and firmly establishes the premises of their relationship. Many of the comments made in this first exchange (which, incidentally, was not meant for publication),[10] reappear in his later statements to and about Luther. Erasmus expressed concern that humanism was being linked with the reform movement and voiced fears that the New Learning would suffer by association. Luther's publications gave the scholastic theologians 'an opening to suppress both humane studies – for which they have a burning hatred, as likely to stand in the way of her majesty Queen Theology, whom they value much more than they do Christ – and myself at the same time.'[11] Erasmus insisted that he had not read Luther's works and was unwilling to judge their contents, and he strained the credulity of his readers by maintaining for years to come that he had no time to peruse Luther's writings, except in snatches.

In his very first communication to Luther, Erasmus made the statement, which became the watchword of many of his followers: 'I keep myself uncommitted', he said, 'in hopes of being able to do more for the revival of good literature.' This remarkable explanation informs us about his priorities and perhaps gave rise to Melanchthon's unfavourable comparison of him with Luther. Erasmus seemed preoccupied with the fate of the humanistic movement and frequently voiced fears about the New Learning becoming entangled in the religious question. In the letter to Luther he also struck a critical note that remained a constant in his discussion of the religious debate. Whatever Luther was teaching (of which Erasmus purported to be ignorant), he had not chosen the right method of teaching. Erasmus had two pieces of advice for Luther. First, the reformer was too aggressive. 'One gets further by courtesy and moderation than by clamour.' He advises Luther to disguise his accusations by using allegory, to refrain from attacking persons in high places and exercise diplomacy, laying the blame for any abusive practice on their underlings. He wants Luther to be persuasive rather than assertive.

Perhaps his enemies were guilty of aggression as well, but they were 'better ignored than refuted'. Secondly, Erasmus advises Luther to be patient, to aim at reform rather than revolution. Certain undesirable practices were too well established to be rooted out at once.[12] Although a critical tone pervades Erasmus's letter, his courteous assurance that Luther needed no instruction from him ('I am not instructing you to do this, only to do what you do always') was interpreted by some readers as an overall endorsement of the reformer.

Both this letter and another addressed to Albert, Archbishop of Mainz, in which Erasmus clarified his views on Luther, were published without his authorization. In the letter to the archbishop, Erasmus repeats the themes that appear in his first letter to Luther and continue to crop up in his comments on the reformation movement over the next five years: the wish to remain neutral; the fear that humanistic studies would suffer by association with Luther's cause; and strong disapproval for the aggressive methods used by both Luther and his critics. Erasmus assured the archbishop that he had had no time to read Luther's books 'except for dipping into some of them here and there' and that he wished to remain on the sidelines. 'I do not accuse Luther, I do not defend him'; 'I should not be willing to write anything in that field myself, nor do I claim to possess sufficient learning to be ready to keep an eye on what other men write.' His area of expertise was philology, and he feared that the theologians who 'have long resented the new blossoming of the humanities and the ancient tongues, and the revival of the authors of Antiquity' would seize on this opportunity and 'tie up the ancient tongues and the humanities and Reuchlin and Luther and even myself in the same parcel, their distinctions being as much at sea as their deductions. To begin with, what can liberal studies have in common with a question of religious faith? And then what have I in common with Reuchlin or with Luther?'[13]

Erasmus no doubt expected that such disclaimers would discourage people from associating him with Luther or the humanities with the reformation movement. After all, he noted, Luther's 'acquaintance with the humanities was but slender'. He seemed at cross purposes, however, when he continued his letter freely criticizing the practices of the Catholic Church. Such criticism would certainly have invited comparison with Luther. Christians, Erasmus said, were burdened with man-made rules, the tyranny of the scholastic theologians and mendicant orders. Indulgences were hawked in terms one 'could not stomach'; religion centred on the observance of rites, encouraging a 'more than Jewish ceremonial'; Church leaders neglected their pastoral duties and were motivated by ambition and financial gain. Luther had voiced similar complaints. A discerning reader, however, would have recognized that Erasmus criticized abuses without challenging doctrine. He denounced the commercial practices of the papal court, but expressed respect for the office of the pope and acknowledged his primacy – a doctrine soon to be attacked by Luther. The point Erasmus wished to make in his letter was the need for instruction rather than coercion. Authority or authoritarianism would not carry the day. Luther was admittedly 'intemperate', but his enemies were intent on nothing but 'compulsion, or destruction and annihilation . . . this is to play the butcher not the theologian'. Projecting his own attitude on Luther, Erasmus insisted that the reformer had put forward subjects 'for discussion', that he 'wished for instruction' and 'submitted himself to the judgement of the Apostolic See'. While this is hardly a realistic assessment of Luther's stand, we must remember that Erasmus wrote those words in 1520, when the schismatic nature of Luther's teaching was not entirely clear. That point was established only at his trial at the Diet of Worms in 1521.

A heightened sense of caution and a dawning consciousness that Luther's teaching might lead to schism is evident, however, in the next epistolary exchange of August 1520. The main themes we have already noted make their appearance once again. Erasmus expressed reluctance to take sides and to go on record with his views: 'I am not the right man, my dear Luther, to give you advice . . . you are too good a scholar for [me], a man with too little learning to be able to form an opinion about you.' Humanism was bound to suffer in the process: 'Conspiracies go on everywhere against the authors of the "new learning"'; 'more prudence and moderation' was wanted.[14] Erasmus proposed a truce: he would not attack Luther, and was asking in turn that Luther refrain from involving his name in his affairs. He put it diplomatically: 'I shall not oppose your policy, for fear that, if it is inspired by the spirit of Christ, I may be opposing Christ.' He would prefer not to have his name mentioned because 'undoubtedly it harms me and does your cause no good.' By naming names, Luther will cast suspicion on men, 'who could be more use to you if they were left alone'.[15] We see here the mixture of practical and ideological arguments, which was anathema to Luther and earned Erasmus the reputation of being a time-server. At the time Erasmus was under considerable pressure to abandon his neutrality. As he told the bishop of Utrecht, he wanted 'nothing to do with this miserable business. However, there is actually a bishopric waiting for me, if I will attack Luther in print.'[16] Such boasts would come to haunt him later, when his enemies alleged that he remained in the Catholic fold because he had been bribed by Rome.

In spite of his professed reluctance to engage in the debate, Erasmus published three short tracts on the Luther question in 1520. He commented on the condemnation of Luther by the Louvain theologians (*Acts of the Louvain University against Luther*); he summed up his own position on the Luther affair in *Axiomata or Brief Notes . . . on the Cause of Martin Luther* (1520); and he offered more specific counsel on resolving the religious debate in a third memorandum, *Advice Composed by a Person Seriously Wishing . . . for the Peace of the Church*. In these documents, for the first time, Erasmus brings epistemological considerations to bear on the Luther question. He comments on the method of determining the doctrinal truth, that is, of establishing the doctrinally correct interpretation of Scripture, calling repeatedly for a two-step procedure. The first step was the collection of evidence on both sides of the question. The second step was an analysis or comparison of the evidence, leading to a resolution. If the evidence was clear, it allowed a decision based on the rules of logic; if it was ambiguous, the decision must be based on the authoritative teaching of the Church.

In 1521 Luther took his stand at the Diet of Worms and was subsequently placed under the ban. Shortly after the publication of the Edict, Erasmus wrote to Justus Jonas, once more discussing the Luther question. In his letter he insisted that his 'attitude towards Luther was the same as it used to be. It has not changed.' He repeated many points he made in his earlier correspondence, including the increasingly implausible assertion that he 'had not yet had the leisure to read' Luther's books. He reiterated that he had no intention of writing 'in the service of any party; I serve Christ, who belongs to us all.'[17] He explained once more that he strongly disapproved of Luther's radical methods. His attempts to uproot long-established practices were bound to lead to subversion. 'It would have been wise to soften a naturally painful subject by the courtesy of one's handling than to pile one cause of hatred on another.'[18] The letter to Jonas, then, contained the familiar themes: protestations of neutrality, appeals for moderation, and concern for the fate of the humanities. In addition, however, Erasmus introduced the subject that made its appearance in the tracts published in 1520: the quest for truth and its management and dissemination. The subject became the philosophical divide separating Erasmus from Luther and dominated his polemic with the reformer over free will in 1524, when the two men finally made their dispute public.

In the letter to Jonas, Erasmus made a number of important statements on truth and on the teaching authority of the Church. If the Church 'is not held together by concord', he wrote, 'it has ceased to deserve the name of Church'.[19] What may appear at first blush as conventional regret that a religious peace could not be achieved at the Diet of Worms contains on closer inspection a statement that is significant for our understanding of Erasmus's ecclesiology. In his view, concord marked and defined the true Church, which was the recipient of God's word and the guardian of spiritual truth. Pursuing the subject further, Erasmus stated that the authority to interpret the Word of God and to pronounce on the truth was given to few men. Some doctrinal questions were destined to remain unsettled and should therefore not be discussed in the hearing of the laity. Quibbling and quarrelling theologians created a climate of doubt with their 'wilful obscurity'. Instructions to the common people must be clear. Questions of doctrine were, so to speak, 'mysteries reserved for the initiate'; they were the domain of academic theologians.[20] There was no need to involve the people in such questions.

In a key statement on the subject of disseminating the truth, Erasmus writes: 'A prudent steward will husband the truth – bring it out, I mean, when the business requires it and bring it out so much as is requisite and bring out for every man what is appropriate for him.'[21] Luther was wrong to discuss before the common people issues that should be handled by scholars. In addressing the people, 'it is right for truth to remain unspoken, and everywhere the time, the manner and the recipients of its publication are of great importance'.[22] We see in these two statements the vocabulary of relativism. Time, mode and person are variants in determining correct speech or action. Erasmus uses similar language in a letter to the inquisitor Jacob Hoogstraten, when he notes that the Church should use its teaching authority to interpret the Word of God 'as time and circumstance may require'.[23] Plato granted to the guardians of his ideal state the right to promulgate white lies if the welfare of the people demanded it. Erasmus does not go as far as endorsing lies, but he acknowledges the usefulness of husbanding the truth. With surprising candour he says: 'We need a sort of holy cunning; we must be time-servers, but without betraying the treasure of gospel truth from which our lost standards of public morality can be restored.'[24]

Although calls for moderation and accommodation prevail in Erasmus's advice concerning the religious debate and give it the appearance of a political or diplomatic exercise, relativism and a sceptical epistemology form a subtext. To justify relativism, Erasmus points to Christ and the apostles as models. Christ 'says one thing to the multitudes, who are somewhat thick-witted, and another to his disciples'. Peter held back explanations, 'reserving the mystery [of Christ's nature] until its proper time'. Paul became 'all things to all men' by twisting or withholding evidence that would not have been convincing.[25] By contrast, Erasmus condemns the positivist logic embraced by the scholastics, who settled every doctrinal question with subtle arguments that were unconvincing and constituted merely a formal victory in an academic setting. He contrasts their method with the patristic theology, a flexible and persuasive *theologia rhetorica*. The Fathers did not aim at winning an argument but at restoring consensus, which is a defining quality of truth and of the Church in which God has vested the truth. In his proposal for a peaceful resolution of the Luther affair, Erasmus therefore calls for a commission of scholars and men of moral integrity to examine the evidence and pronounce judgement with authority. In a contemporary letter to Cardinal Campeggi, Erasmus returns once again to the subject of truth, and to the expedience of telling or withholding the truth depending on the circumstances. 'It is always of the first importance how timely, how opportune and how well judged your production of it is.'[26]

After the formal condemnation of Luther, pressure increased for Erasmus to abandon his neutrality and oppose Luther in print. Pope Leo X personally encouraged him to take up the pen. 'Never was the time more opportune or the cause more just for setting your erudition and your powers of mind against the impious.'[27] Erasmus's reluctance was seen as delaying tactics and threatened to make him persona non grata with partisans in both camps. 'I am a heretic to both sides', he wrote in 1522.[28] Pope Adrian VI, who succeeded Leo on his death in 1521, again urged Erasmus to make his position clear in print: 'Employ in an attack on these new heresies the literary skill with which a generous providence has endowed you.'[29] There is evidence that Erasmus was planning to write three dialogues on the Luther question, as he told his friend Johann Botzheim in December 1523. Dialogue was the genre of choice for sceptics since it allowed the simultaneous projection of different points of view without the necessity of providing a definite solution. Erasmus used the device many times, notably in the *Colloquies*, often leaving the discussion open-ended by allowing his fictitious protagonists to plead exhaustion or to promise a continuation of the discussion another day. The planned trilogy of dialogues never appeared, but the colloquies 'An Examination Concerning the Faith' and 'The Fish Diet', published in 1524 and 1526 respectively, may be based on material earmarked for it.

The dialogues dealt with controversial doctrines held by the reformers and raised speculation that the characters 'Aulus' and 'Barbatus' represented Erasmus and Luther respectively.

One final epistolary exchange between Erasmus and Luther preceded their polemic of 1524. Erasmus had asked for a truce, and Luther noted that he had complied with his request and kept silent. Although he felt stung by Erasmus's criticism, he observed their gentlemen's agreement.[30] 'Because he pretends publicly not to be my enemy', he wrote to Oecolampadius in 1523, 'I too pretend not to understand his cunning.'[31] In April 1524 Luther sought reassurance from Erasmus that he in turn would maintain the truce. 'The one thing to be afraid of was that you might be persuaded by my enemies to attack my opinions in your public work, and that I should then be obliged to resist you to your face . . . I shall continue to restrain [my pen] until you come out into the open.' At the same time he declared defiantly that the reformation movement had nothing to fear from Erasmus and would succeed 'even if Erasmus opposes it with all his powers'. Luther seemed to reply to Erasmus's slighting remark about his lack of humanistic learning by pointing out the latter's limitations. He had done much for the progress of the humanities, but it would be better if he stuck to his own field of expertise. God had endowed him with special gifts in philology, but not yet infused him with the zeal and spirit of a reformer. Luther accepted the fact that Erasmus wanted to remain a spectator, 'if that is the best thing you can do'. He warned him, however, not to join the enemy camp. 'Do not publish any attack on me, and I shall refrain from attacking you.'[32] Neither Luther nor Erasmus in his reply mentioned that the intention to keep their disagreements private had been foiled by the unauthorized publication in January 1523 of a private letter from Luther to a physician in Leipzig.[33] In that letter Luther repeated that he was willing to refrain from attacking Erasmus publicly, as long as Erasmus in turn kept to the terms of their truce.

Their relationship now entered a new phase. In his last extant letter to Luther, Erasmus noted that he would like nothing better than to remain a spectator, but the attacks he suffered from all sides made it impossible. Catholics accused him of being in league with Luther, while the latter's own followers denounced him in libellous pamphlets as a hypocrite. Thus he was compelled to take a stand. The letter containing that announcement was dated 8 May 1524.[34] In early September *De libero arbitrio diatribe sive collatio* (Diatribe or Comparison on Free Will) appeared. In a letter to Melanchthon, Erasmus justified his decision to write against Luther. 'You will wonder', he wrote, 'why I published my book on the freedom of the will. I had to fight off three ranks of enemies.' First, the enemies of the New Learning were trying to ruin the humanities by linking the humanists (and Erasmus in particular) with Lutheranism. Secondly, Catholic leaders put him under pressure to write against Luther, and Luther's followers attacked him as a coward for remaining on the sidelines. Thirdly, thanks to unauthorized publications of their correspondence, it was now public knowledge that Luther had offered to 'restrain his pen in writing of me if I keep quiet'. As a result, his silence would be construed as collusion with Luther. The combination of circumstances had made it impossible for him to remain silent. However, he had carefully refrained from the kind of emotional and abusive language commonly used by polemicists. His treatise was a sober and scholarly investigation of a question central to theology.[35]

For his investigation Erasmus had chosen a doctrinal question that separated Catholics from reformers: the question of free will. Catholics accepted the existence of free will, but made moral decisions a cooperative act, in which God aided the weak but willing human being. Lutherans rejected the concept of free will, and insisting on the total dependence of the individual on divine grace. Another important issue was behind the arguments of the disputants: the question of the clarity or obscurity of Scripture. It was a question that occasionally surfaced and overshadowed the doctrinal question. Thus hermeneutics were 'almost more to the point than the disputation itself', as Erasmus noted.[36] Indeed, Erasmus chose the subject because it afforded him an excellent opportunity to showcase the method of investigation he wanted theologians to adopt. He meant the work to be an *epideixis*, a display of method. Luther's reply, *De servo arbitrio* (On the Bondage of the Will, 1525), acknowledged the methodological thrust of Erasmus's work. He entered into the discussion, but attempted to discount its philosophical import and to depict it as an *epideixis* of rhetorical powers.

In his introduction Erasmus explains that his method consists of 'juxtaposing various scriptural texts and arguments to illuminate the truth'. He anticipates the outcome: ambiguity, which forces him to fall back on the verdict of the Church. At the same time, he voices his disapproval of positivism:

I take so little pleasure in assertions that I will gladly seek refuge in scepticism whenever this is allowed by the inviolable authority of Holy Scripture and the Church's decrees; to these decrees I willingly submit my judgement in all things, whether I fully understand what the Church commands or not. I prefer, indeed, to have this cast of mind than that which I see characterizes certain others, so that they are uncontrollably attached to an opinion and . . . twist whatever they read in Scripture to support the view they have embraced once for all.[37]

Erasmus himself proposes to approach doctrinal questions without preconceived notions, examining the evidence on both sides. After listing biblical passages for and against free will, he concludes that they do not provide a clear answer to the question at hand. He therefore withholds judgement, that is, he does not (and cannot) base his judgement on scriptural evidence, and instead accepts the teaching authority of the Church. Luther wishes to establish doctrine *sola scriptura*, on the basis of Scripture alone. Erasmus's list of relevant passages is designed to show the futility of Luther's procedure and to demonstrate the obscurity of the sacred text. The obscurity of the text, Erasmus points out, explains the discrepancy among the interpretations offered by exegetes over the ages. Holy Scripture is clear on matters essential to salvation, but it also contains matters 'into which God did not intend us to penetrate very far'. In Erasmus's view, the question of free will was among the subjects that were impenetrable to human intelligence. It was therefore better to refrain from assertions concerning free will than 'to define what passes the scope of human thought'.[38] Nor was it a subject fit for public discussion. Here Erasmus once again touches on the topic of husbanding the truth and uses the terms of relativism. Discussing free will before the people may be lawful, 'but it is not expedient to do so in front of anyone, at any time, in any way'.[39]

Continuing his remarks on method, Erasmus turns to the nature of the evidence to be taken into consideration. He agrees with Luther that scriptural evidence is of principal importance, but insists that one must also listen to the opinion of learned commentators and 'the consensus of the very many centuries' emerging from them. The debate was not about Scripture itself, he noted, 'the quarrel was over its meaning'. If the text was as clear as Luther claimed, what need was there for exegetes or for the gift of prophecy? If the text was obscure, as Erasmus claimed and had shown in his juxtaposition of seemingly contradictory evidence, who was qualified to make a pronouncement? Who was inspired by God to provide the correct interpretation? 'How shall we test the spirits? By Learning? There are scholars on both sides. By behaviour? On both sides there are sinners . . . What am I to do if many people assert different opinions, every one of them swearing that he has the Spirit?'[40] Erasmus does not immediately answer these questions. He merely notes that he makes no claims for himself and therefore offers no answers. 'I discuss rather than dispute the matter.' He compares his position to that of Nicodemus or Gamaliel, who 'suspended his judgement . . . till the outcome of the affair should show in what spirit it was being directed'.[41]

In his reply, the *Bondage of the Will*, Luther answered Erasmus's methodological explanation defiantly. He was not content with discussing the issue: 'Rather, I have made and am still making assertions.' He scoffed at Erasmus's sceptical approach. There was no room for sceptics in the present debate. What was needed were 'asserters twice as unyielding as the Stoics themselves'. This was the method proper for Christians. 'This is how a Christian will speak . . . I will not only consistently adhere to and assert sacred writings everywhere and in all its parts, but I also wish to be as certain as possible in things that are not vital and that lie outside of Scripture. For what is more miserable than uncertainty?' He trumped Erasmus's reasoning with the assertion that 'the Holy Spirit is no sceptic'.[42]

The term 'sceptic' carried considerable baggage in the sixteenth century. Martin Schoock, a seventeenth-century historian of scepticism and, I believe, the first modern author daring enough to undertake such a task, declared that scepticism invariably led to atheism. 'We must not be surprised, if there seem to be rather few proponents and disseminators of scepticism', he wrote. In his opinion, scepticism was alive but its proponents had gone underground. The rejection of scepticism in the Renaissance formed part of the ongoing dispute over the use (and the dangers) of pagan philosophical writings for Christians. Both Aristotle and Plato had long been Christianized and the former was in fact the principal author read in universities and the mainstay of scholasticism. Platonism had been given a Christian sheen by Marsiglio Ficino and his followers. Scepticism, however, was not susceptible to the same processes. In the eyes of the theologians it remained incompatible with religion. Yet the scholastic method of *sic et non*, of arguing on both sides of a question before passing judgement, was essentially a sceptical method. The scholastic theologians, however, avoided the unpalatable, doubt-inducing suspension of judgement, which was the classic sceptic's solution to logically insoluble problems. They concluded disputations with magisterial assertions, cutting the Gordian knot with an academic sword, so to speak. Humanists, who employed the sceptical method as a rhetorical strategy, often camouflaged it by using dialogue, which allowed the suspension of judgement without further explanation. Neither humanists nor scholastics spoke of their method as a form of scepticism, presumably to avoid the odium adhering to that philosophy. Erasmus was one of the few men who openly spoke in favour of scepticism and attempted to Christianize it, that is, to make it a legitimate epistemological approach in the eyes of his contemporaries.

In the *Hyperaspistes* (A Shield-bearing Warrior, 1526), in which he followed up on Luther's *Bondage of the Will*, Erasmus clarified the sense in which he used the term scepticism. Rejecting Luther's 'slanderous' equation of scepticism with atheism, Erasmus explained: 'First I myself explicitly exclude from scepticism whatever is set forth [i.e. clearly stated] in Sacred Scripture or whatever has been handed down to us by the authority of the Church.' In cases in which such a verdict has been rendered scepticism is inappropriate. The verdict of the Church turns the disputed question into an article of faith. 'On these points I am so far from desiring or having a sceptical outlook that I would not hesitate to face death to uphold them.' But he was talking about matters as yet under discussion. 'Questions on which the Church has not yet made a clear pronouncement . . . are subject to the attitude of scepticism.' Once the Church has rendered its verdict, 'I have no use for human arguments but rather follow the decision of the Church and cease to be a sceptic . . . I am not dealing with Scripture but with conflicts, that is, controversial issues.'[43]

The Erasmian sceptic, then, is a man who 'shrinks from rash definitions, not from assertions'. Free will was a subject on which the Church had rendered a verdict. There was room for the sceptical method but not for the classic sceptical conclusion, suspended judgement. The concept of free will has been endorsed 'by an overwhelming consensus and the Church has clearly defined it as something not to be disputed but to be believed.' The purpose of any further discussion was to contribute to a better understanding of the teaching of the Church.[44]

It is clear from Erasmus's statements that the type of scepticism he advocates is a corollary of his Christian humanism. He takes his departure from a classical concept and successfully blends it with Christian thought, or more specifically, tailors it to his own Catholic beliefs. He creates a variant on the Ciceronian or academic scepticism, which substituted plausibility for certain truth to avoid the intellectual paralysis caused by suspension of judgement. Erasmus refers to academic scepticism when he first touches on the subject in the prolegomena to his edition of the New Testament. Criticizing the scholastic practice of providing a magisterial answer to all questions, he writes:

Why is it necessary for the theologian to answer with certainty everyone's slightest question? . . . There are things that it is rather impious to investigate. There are things that can remain unknown without detriment to our salvation. There are things, about which scholars may remain in doubt and, like the academics, withhold their opinion rather than pronounce a verdict.[45]

There is a place for the academic principle of plausibility in Erasmus's scheme. He expands on this point in the *Hyperaspistes*. Once the Church has spoken, the believer accepts her verdict because it flows from divine inspiration. Arriving at this verdict, however, was a process involving several stages. A person emerging from darkness into light, he says, is only gradually able to make out the shape of things, as his eyes adjust to the light. 'What was obscure before gradually begins to be clear to us.'[46] In the same manner, some doctrinal questions could not be immediately settled. The truth was perceived only after a thorough search and in the fullness of time. In the meantime, the Christian sceptic might accept plausible solutions.

In Erasmus's view, accepting the verdict of the Church in cases where scriptural evidence was ambiguous provided a safety-net. It was sometimes difficult to decide in whom the prophetic spirit of God was vested, he said, taking aim at Luther's claim to inspiration. 'It is safer to follow public authority than the opinion of someone or other . . . who boasts of his own conscience and spirit.'[47] The Christian sceptic, then, relies on long-standing consensus and the authority of the institutional Church to overcome the logical impasse created by ambiguous evidence. This is a quintessential Catholic solution. Catholics held that doctrine rested on the twin pillars of Scripture and tradition, whereas the reformers embraced the principle of *sola scriptura*, by Scripture alone. Luther insisted on the clarity of Scripture; Erasmus contended that the disagreements among the reformers contradicted this claim. Luther, too, settled questions of interpretation by authority rather than logical or philological arguments, he argued. They differed only in one point. Erasmus relied on the teaching authority of the Church; Luther vested this authority in himself.[48]

Explaining the process of discovering and disseminating the truth, Erasmus once again uses the language of relativism. Comparing the process of finding the doctrinal truth with a judicial inquiry, he notes that a judge will weigh circumstances if the evidence put forward by the parties is equally convincing. 'Circumstances are usually taken into account . . . some allowance is made for age, dignity and authority'. Similarly, the Christian sceptic, when faced with convincing arguments on both sides of a doctrinal question, takes into consideration time and authority. He will consider long-standing practices, the standing of the scholars defending each side, and the authority commanded by those pronouncing on doctrine. Time and authority, Erasmus says, support the idea of freedom of the will. It is a concept 'approved down through many centuries and confirmed finally by the public decision of the Church'.[49]

Discussing the method of teaching doctrine and preaching it from the pulpit, Erasmus once again professes himself a relativist. The principles of *aptum et decorum* must guide the speaker. He must take into consideration the circumstances and pay attention to expedience when delivering a sermon or a lecture. This, Erasmus says, was the approach of St Paul, and indeed, of Christ himself. Paul was aware of what was 'in season and out of season' and declared self-consciously: 'All things are permitted to me but not all things are expedient.' Christ endorsed this idea when he said: 'There is a time for speaking and a time for remaining silent.'[50] In his *Bondage of the Will*, Luther had taken umbrage at Erasmus's relativism and protested against the absurdity of the formulation 'it is not expedient to [teach doctrine] to all persons whatsoever, at any time whatsoever, in any way whatsoever'. He labelled Erasmus a hypocrite, toadying to those in power. What, then, he asked in a tone of mockery, was the right audience, time, and mode of speaking? Erasmus protested against Luther's 'clumsy jests' and lectured him in turn. A preacher tempers his speech so as not to provoke powerful men needlessly and thereby harm the cause of the gospel. That is what he meant by adapting the speech to the audience. 'When there is no hope of success but the only result is to create an uproar, the matter should be put off until a better occasion arises.' That is what he meant by observing the right time. 'But as for the method of teaching, it is drawn from all the circumstances and cannot be entirely prescribed because it arises and varies with the case at hand and what is appropriate for each case is left to the prudence of the steward [of the truth].'[51]

Examining the dynamics of the relationship between Erasmus and Luther in light of the developments between 1519 and 1525, we find it shaped by a mixture of motives and concerns. At the most mundane level, Erasmus feared to give offence to the authorities; as a man of letters he was concerned that the humanities would suffer by association with the reformers; as a lover of peace and order he wished for a settlement of the religious question by accommodation; and as a Christian sceptic he needed consensus as a decision-making tool. Erasmus's consistent disapproval of the radical methods employed by Luther and his fear of a schism may have been rooted in his personal style. He preferred diplomacy to confrontation. It may also have contained a strategic element: the desire to retain the patronage of Catholic rulers and prelates. But these motives were not the mainsprings of Erasmus's attitude toward Luther. His actions (and his initial reluctance to act) were determined primarily by intellectual concerns: a sceptical epistemology and the desire to protect humanistic studies from the opprobrium adhering to the reformers. The former prevented him from making a personal decision on doctrinal questions for which he could find no unequivocal answer in Scripture and obliged him to fall back on tradition and authority, a requirement inclining him to embrace Catholicism. The latter involved him in the hopeless quest of separating philology from exegesis, which led him to adopt a wilful blindness and to resort to implausible disclaimers. While Erasmus's scepticism and its frequent corollary, relativism, was logically defensible, the rhetorical sleights he performed in defence of philology were not. Neither scepticism nor rhetorical stratagems were popular in a time characterized by a partisan spirit, when absolute loyalty to the cause was demanded and strident and unvarnished language was the chosen means to demonstrate commitment.

Epilogue
The remains of the day:
Erasmianism today

In the chapters of this book I have dealt with various aspects of Erasmian thought. It remains to consider whether any one aspect may be regarded as the essence of Erasmianism. The designation 'Erasmian' is not modern, but was coined in the sixteenth century. The very use of the term suggests that his contemporaries had already formed a concept of what constituted the core of Erasmus's teachings, what was typically 'Erasmian'. The famous Catholic apologist Johann Eck may have been the first to use the epithet when he wrote in 1520: 'All scholars are convinced Erasmians, except for a few monks and pseudo-theologians.' At that time Eck was an admirer of Erasmus. The letter is full of conventional flattery and rhetorical flourishes. We cannot therefore expect a precise definition of the term, but Eck's 'Erasmians' were presumably men who emulated the qualities for which he expressed admiration: 'all-round learning and copious powers of expression'.[1] In 1574 the Swiss chronicler Johann Kessler used the term 'Erasmian' in the same comprehensive sense: 'Whatever is skilled, polished, learned and wise is called Erasmian', he wrote.[2] Again, the wider context of Kessler's remarks suggests that he was admiring Erasmus's scope of learning, but especially his language skills and rhetorical powers. It was in a similar sense that the Louvain theologian Frans Titelmans used the term in 1530. Students of the humanities, he wrote, were called 'Erasmians' because Erasmus was 'either the leader and patron or the founder of their studies'.[3] The reformer Conradus Pellicanus, however, related that some readers saw Erasmians in much more specific terms. In their view, Erasmians were locked in battle with members of the religious orders – a notion that appears obliquely also in Eck's letter. Pellicanus, however, did not endorse that perception of Erasmianism. He believed that men who disapproved of

106

monasticism in principle and claimed that they had taken their cue from Erasmus's writings, were using his name in vain. They were 'impostors' who put a crude interpretation on Erasmus's finely nuanced words and attributed to him a radicalism which he had never advocated. Erasmus, then, was an early victim of the misinterpretations and generalizations usually dogging famous men, whose name has become a byword. Not surprisingly, the search for the meaning of 'Erasmian' and 'Erasmianism' remains a scholarly quest today.

The difficulty of pinpointing the essence of Erasmianism has been acknowledged both in his own time and in later historiography. Luther famously called Erasmus an 'eel, whom no one can grasp', and in the late nineteenth century Thomas Martin Lindsay, a historian of the reformation, noted that Erasmus had 'the ingenuity of a cuttlefish to conceal himself and his real opinions'.[4] In my generation, Lisa Jardine pointed out Erasmus's 'purposive' narrative,[5] that is, the self-fashioning purpose of his writing; and the title of Léon Halkin's biography, *Erasmus ex Erasmo*, similarly suggests that we know of Erasmus only what he was willing to give away. As Bruce Mansfield put it rather well, his public image was the result of a 'high degree of calculation and of career planning'.[6] The descriptive phrases used by these scholars carry a negative connotation, impinging on Erasmus's veracity. As we have seen, however, his concept of the truth was closely bound up with his scepticism, and the liberty he takes in casting himself in the character appropriate to the circumstances at hand and of highlighting different facets of his personality, depending on the context wanted, are corollaries of his scepticism.

Indeed one may rightly ask if scepticism, relativism and their inherent shifts of thought should be accepted as the defining mark of Erasmianism, or at any rate as the quality that keeps him in the eye of the modern reader. Clearly Erasmianism in its earliest meaning, relating to style, is no longer a drawing card, since Latin has ceased to be the international language of scholars and the majority of readers today approach Erasmus through the medium of translation. Yet the content of his writings remains relevant. His *Praise of Folly* has never been out of print. There are two ongoing editions of his *Opera omnia*, one in Latin, the other in English. A journal, *The Erasmus of Rotterdam Yearbook*, is exclusively dedicated to Erasmian scholarship, and in the 1960s and 1970s, before electronic searches became possible, Jean-Claude Margolin published three bibliographical volumes, documenting the scholarly industry that has grown up around Erasmus.

There is some indication of the historical appeal of Erasmus's scepticism from the eighteenth century onward. In his own time, the methodology of doubt was an underground philosophy. Its champions kept a low profile to avoid prosecution by inquisitorial tribunals. Both Catholics and Protestants perceived scepticism as the precursor of atheism. During the Enlightenment, however, scepticism underwent a re-evaluation. It was now associated with rationalism. Wilhelm Dilthey went as far as calling Erasmus the 'Voltaire of the sixteenth century' and the 'founder of religious rationalism'.[7] It is well that Dilthey used the adjective 'religious' to qualify Erasmian rationalism. As we have seen, he did not terminate enquiries into doctrinal questions with *epoche*, as a purely rational process required, but took refuge in the authority of the Church. In his denial of the power of the human intellect to discern the absolute truth, Erasmus came closer to mysticism than to rationalism. The mystic admits his impotence and commits himself to God; the rationalist admits only that his means of perception are insufficient *at the time* and leaves open the possibility of a future breakthrough. The rationalist, furthermore, will pursue truth aggressively and to the limits of his ability; Erasmus regarded pursuing the truth beyond the limits set by the Church as unwarranted inquisitiveness or *curiositas*. Such heavily qualified 'rationalism' finds little praise in the twenty-first century. Erasmus's scepticism, however, is linked with other goals regarded desirable today. Liberal thinkers favour tolerance over prejudice, diplomacy and accommodation over militarism, ecumenism and inclusiveness over confessionalization. These political virtues, which have a high currency in Western society, are (rightly or wrongly) associated with Erasmus. It is certainly correct to associate Erasmus with aspects of tolerance, diplomacy and accommodation, but it is wrong to associate him with the full range of meanings these words have today. His tolerance did not extend to views considered heterodox by the Catholic Church; he harboured anti-Semitic thoughts and subscribed to the discrimination against women common in his time, and he would not have embraced multiculturalism or sanctioned a diversity of lifestyles. What he had in mind is what his age called *civilitas*, civility at the personal and communal level, or courtesy coupled with goodwill. 'Good manners and civility' are the qualities Philip Melanchthon associated with Erasmus, as we have seen. In the same vein, the jurist Udalricus Zasius praised Erasmus as a moderate, who promoted 'peace, civility and goodwill'.[8] The twentieth-century Dutch historian Johan Huizinga translated these qualities into 'gentleness, kindliness, moderation', which he also, by the way, ascribed to his own Dutch people.[9] This romancing of Erasmus (and the Dutch people) may not be entirely justifiable but is, at any rate, more tenable than the unqualified association of Erasmus with pacifism. A number of modern scholars, among them Marcel Bataillon, Cornelis Augustijn and Nicolette Mout, have protested against the facile identification of Erasmus's *civilitas* with shallow feel-good concepts that lend themselves to being printed on T-shirts.[10] A much more sophisticated appreciation of Erasmian *civilitas* is offered by Ralf Dahrendorf, who characterized it as 'leise Passion der Vernunft', the soft passion of reason.[11] He sees it as the quality that allows people to avoid the pitfalls of extremism and believes that it is an antidote to the political radicalism of fascists and communists. Like Huizinga, Dahrendorf associates this quality with a nation, in this case the English, who, he says, stand for the virtues embodied by Erasmus: 'a humane and peaceful attitude, civility, liberty, equality, stability, tolerance, and respect for the rights of the individual'. Whatever one may think of Dahrendorf's characterization, it is devoutly to be hoped that reading Erasmus's works will inspire such virtues and make Erasmians of us all.

Notes

For abbreviations used in the Notes, please see Select Bibliography.

INTRODUCTION

1. *CWE* 71, 92.
2. *Erasmus Reader*, 128, 136.
3. *CWE* Ep. 1183: 41–2.
4. *Erasmus of Christendom* vii.
5. Allen Ep. 2445: 137.

CHAPTER 1

1. *CWE* Ep. 1437. The warning was in Greek, the language that formed a special bond between members of the humanistic republic of letters.
2. Allen Ep. 1581: 897–99.
3. Ibid., 71.
4. *CWE* Ep. 1437: 2–3.
5. The text is in *Erasmus Reader*, 15–20; and in *CWE* 4: 400–10. A similar sketch, Ep. 447 'To Lambertus Grunnius', was written in 1516 for the purpose of obtaining a papal dispensation.
6. *CWE* Ep. 447: 9.
7. H. Vredeveld, 'The Ages of Erasmus and the Year of his Birth', *Renaissance Quarterly* 46 (1993) 753–809.

8. *Erasmus Reader*, 16.

9. *CWE* Ep. 447: 246–50.

10. Erasmus obtained two dispensations: see *CWE* Ep. 187 from Pope Julius II, 1506 and the fuller dispensation in Ep. 317 from Leo X, 1516. Erasmus needed the dispensations to qualify for benefices at Aldington (a gift of Archbishop William of Warham, 1512) and Courtrai (1516).

11. *CWE* Ep. 517: 9–10.

12. *Erasmus Reader*, 17.

13. Ibid., 22.

14. *CWE* Ep. 447: 178–80.

15. Erasmus took a dim view of their motives. He acknowledged that entering the Church was a 'convenient vehicle for the feeding of many creatures who would otherwise starve to death' (*CWE* Ep. 447: 336–7) and commented sarcastically: His guardians thought they 'sacrificed a victim most pleasing to God if [they] should have consigned one of their pupils to the monastic life' (ibid., 99–100).

16. *Erasmus Reader*, 18.

17. Ibid.

18. *CWE* Ep. 296: 48–50.

19. Ibid., 58–61.

20. Ibid., 62.

21. Ibid. 447: 263, but cf. below p. 7, where he blames his health problems on the living conditions at the Collège de Montaigu.

22. *Erasmus Reader*, 18.

23. *CWE* Ep. 517: 7.

24. Ibid. 447: 379–82.

25. Ibid. 348–51.

26. Ibid. 24, 344–57.

27. Quoted E. Rummel, *Erasmus and his Catholic Critics* (Nieuwkoop, 1998) II, 134.

28. *CWE* 25, 136; see his *Defence of the Declamation on Marriage*, *CWE* 71, 85–95.

29. The text is in *CWE* 66.

30. Erasmus uses this phrase in *CWE* Ep. 447: 495.

31. *CWE* 40, 715–16.

32. Cf. J. Farge, 'Erasmus, the University of Paris, and the Prote.. Theology', *Erasmus of Rotterdam Yearbook* 19 (1999) 18–46.

33. *Erasmus Reader*, 19.

34. *CWE* Ep. 64: 82–90, to Thomas Grey.

35. *Erasmus Reader*, 19.

36. *CWE* Ep. 61: 46–54.

37. Ibid., 58: 163–71.

38. Ibid., 70–4.

39. Ibid., Ep. 64: 12–32.

40. *Erasmus Reader*, 19.

41. Ibid.

42. Ibid., 32.

43. The fact that he applied for a papal dispensation in 1506 indicates that he had hopes of receiving a benefice from Warham, but the living of Aldington was bestowed on him only in 1512.

44. *Erasmus Reader*, 19. He was invited by the royal physician Giovanni Battista Boerio to accompany his sons, who were to study in Italy.

45. Ibid., 19–20.

46. Cf. P. Grendler, 'How to get a Degree in Fifteen Days: Erasmus's Doctorate of Theology from the University of Turin', *Erasmus of Rotterdam Yearbook* 18 (1998) 40–69.

47. In 1512 Warham presented him to the living of Aldington in Kent, resigned four months later in exchange for a pension; in 1516 Le Sauvage procured for him a canonry in Courtrai, which Erasmus converted into a pension as well.

48. *Erasmus Reader*, 42.

49. On this subject see P. Bietenholz, 'Haushalten mit der Wahrheit: Erasmus im Dilemma der Kompromissbereitschaft', *Basler Zeitschrift für Altertumskunde* 86 (1986) 9–26; J. Trapmann, 'Erasmus on Lying and Simulation', *Intersections: Yearbook for Early Modern Studies* 2 (2002) 33–46.

50. Quoted by Rummel in *Erasmus and his Catholic Critics* II, 138.

51. Allen I, 70.

52. The list appears in Allen I, 38–42.

53. *Erasmus Reader*, 72, 68.

54. Ibid., 253–4.

55. Ibid., 29.

56. Ibid., 43–4.

57. Ibid., 22–3, 20.

58. Ibid., 48; for a full list of gifts and offers, see *CWE* Ep. 1341A: 1666–751.

59. *Erasmus Reader*, 48.

60. Ibid., 49.

61. See Erasmus's will of 1527, *CWE* 13, 540–50. The provisions for scholarships and dowries are mentioned on p. 547.

CHAPTER 2

1. It was composed in 1489 and published in 1513.

2. *Erasmus Reader*, 23.

3. It was composed as early as 1488 and published in 1520. Text in *CWE* 85, 182–97.

4. *CWE* Ep. 22: 18.

5. Batt eventually became secretary to the town council. He died in 1502.

6. *CWE* 23, 32.

7. Ibid., 44.

8. Ibid., 57–8.

9. Ibid., 68.

10. Ibid., 58.

11. Ibid., 28, 439.

12. Ibid., 441.

13. Ibid., 384, 392.

14. LB IX 664A.

15. *CWE* 28, 439; LB IX 530B.

16. Ibid., 28, 447.

17. The latter appeared first under that title among the prolegomena to his New Testament edition (1516) and was published separately from 1518 on under the title *Ratio verae theologiae*. The text of both works was edited by H. Holborn, *Desiderius Erasmus Roterodamus: Ausgewählte Werke* (Munich, 1933).

18. See, for example, the statistics for Venice in P. Grendler, *Schooling in Renaissance Italy* (Baltimore, MD, 1989), 46.

19. *CWE* Ep. 1233: 112–15.

20. Ibid., 1233: 115–31, 149–52; LB V 615B–E.

21. *CWE* 24, 667.

22. On the three languages, Erasmus says: 'Principal attention should be paid to learning the three languages, Latin, Greek and Hebrew, for it is clear that all the mysteries of Holy Scripture have been handed down in them' (*Ausgewählte Werke*, 151).

23. *CWE* 24, 666.

24. Ibid., 669.

25. Ibid., 679.

26. *Ausgewählte Werke*, 152.

27. Ibid., 158–9.

28. Ibid., 161.

29. See *CWE* Ep. 934, headnote.

30. For a discussion of Mosellanus's speech and Masson's response to him and Erasmus, cf. Rummel, *Erasmus and his Catholic Critics* I, 66–93. Melanchthon's speech, *Sermo habitus apud iuventutem academiae Wittebergensis*, has been edited by H. Stupperich (Gütersloh, 1951) III, 30–42 and translated by R. Keen in *A Melanchthon Reader* (New York, 1988) 47–57.

31. The text of Masson's dialogue has been edited by J. Pijper in *Disputationes contra Lutherum* (The Hague, 1905). The quotation is on p. 60.

32. Ibid., 81.

33. LB IX 922C–D.

34. ASD V-4, 262; V-5, 200.

35. ASD V-4, 44-54.

36. Ibid., 469–70.

37. Ibid., 67–8.

38. *CWE* 39, 251.

39. He wrote a tract on that subject: *Why the Jews Have Lived in Misery for so Long* (1505).

40. Allen Ep. 181: 36–8.

41. Allen Ep. 541:137–8, 148–9.

42. Allen, Ep. 694: 47, 50.

43. On Ricci, see Allen Ep. 549: 36–40; on Adrianus, Ep. 686: 5–8.

44. *CWE* Ep. 1006: 149–50; cf. Ep. 694, a tirade against Pfefferkorn.

45. Ibid., 1333: 323–44; Ep. 1225: 241–2; Ep. 1183: 40–2.

46. ASD V-4, 38; *CWE* 29, 326.

47. ASD V-4, 38–9.

48. *CWE* 24, 666.

49. W. Woodward, *Desiderius Erasmus Concerning the Aim and Method of Education* (New York, 1964), 105.

50. *CWE* 26, 306.

51. *On the Trinity*, 12.

52. *CWE* 26, 311–12, 317.

53. Ibid., 324, 311.

54. Ibid., 300, 314–15; *CWE* 39, 605.

55. *CWE* 26, 319–20: 'A child readily responds to the shameless caresses of his nursemaid and is thus handmoulded by her indecent fondling.'

56. Ibid., 336.

57. Ibid., 306.

58. Ibid., 301–2.

59. Ibid., 318.

60. *CWE* 25, 273.

61. See above, Chapter 1.

62. *CWE* 26, 331.

63. Ibid., 332.

64. Ibid., 299, 342, 313.

65. C. Trinkaus, *In our Image and Likeness* (London, 1970) I, xvii.

CHAPTER 3

1. *CWE* 66, introduction p. xi.

2. Ibid., 124.

3. Ibid., 13–14 (the preface to the 1518 edn of the *Handbook*).

4. Ibid., 16.

5. Ibid., 15.

6. Ibid., 21.

7. Ibid., 173.

8. *CWE* Ep. 61: 51–4, 87–90.

9. *CWE* 63: 13, 21–6.

10. Ibid., 31, 30, 15.

11. Ibid., 65.

12. Ibid., 74. Erasmus uses the terms 'Jews' and 'Judaism' in the sense of literal and mechanical interpretation of the law, which he equated with the Old Testament spirit. See above, chapter 2.

13. *CWE* 66, 35.

14. LB V 65C.

15. LB X 1675B.

16. *Apologia monasticae religionis* (Salamanca, 1528) 12 recto.

17. *CWE* Ep. 1211:36–46.

18. Ibid., lines 66–7, 124–5.

19. Cf. *CWE* 66, 127, where the sentence is translated: 'Being a monk is not a state of holiness but a way of life, which may be beneficial or not according to each person's physical and mental constitution.'

20. For the circumstances, see Chapter 1.

21. The essay was published in 1521. A manuscript copy written before 1513 does not contain the last chapter, thus supplying a *terminus post quem*. See my introduction to the English translation in *CWE* 66, 131–2.

22. *CWE* 66, 173.

23. *Erasmus Reader*, 161–2.

24. *CWE* 39, 471.

25. Ibid., 293.

26. Ibid., 330, 332.

27. Allen Ep. 1456: 21–2, 109. He uses the terms *coactus necessitate* and *manifesta vis* to describe the circumstances (133, 89).

28. Allen Ep. 1887: 6–50.

29. *CWE* 66, 21.

30. Allen Ep. 2771: 49–50, 87–92.

31. E.g. *CWE* 66, 8 (the introduction to the *Handbook*); in *Modus orandi Deum* (Method of praying to God), ASD V-1, 154.

32. *CWE* 61, 7.

33. *Ausgewählte Werke*, 180.

34. *CWE* 66, 61–2.

35. E.g. in the *Handbook*, *CWE* 66, 62: 'convert the riches of Egypt into the adornment of the Lord's temple'.

36. *CWE* Ep. 1039: 245, Ep. 1211: 98; *Ausgewählte Werke* 145, cf. 146: 'Let him grasp and express in his life what Christ taught and demonstrated.'

37. *CWE* Ep. 61: 12, 52–3.

38. *CWE* Ep. 337: 126–8.

39. *Erasmus Reader*, 167–7.

40. *CWE* 40, 1098.

41. Ibid., 39, 91.

42. Ibid., 40, 1100.

43. Ibid., 1101.

44. Ibid., 1104.

45. Ibid., 1105–6.

46. The work first appeared on lists of books banned by the faculty of theology at Paris (from 1544 onwards) and was also listed in the first papal Index of Prohibited Books of 1554/5. It remained on the Index until the end of the nineteenth century. Cf. *CWE* 39, xxxix.

CHAPTER 4

1. The *locus classicus* in the constitutional debate is in Herodotus 3. 80–2.

2. *The Prince*, Chapter 15.

3. *CWE* 27, 217; again at 243.

4. Ibid., 206, 221, 232.

5. *Paraphrase on Romans*, *CWE* 42, 74.

6. *CWE* 27, 231; *CWE* Ep. 858: 304–5.

7. *CWE* 42, 75.

8. See Erasmus, *CWE* 27, 212; elaborating on this parallel, Erasmus follows Seneca (ibid., 225).

9. *CWE* 42, 74.

10. ASD V-4, 202–4.

11. E.g. *CWE* 27, 227; cf. 220.

12. Ibid., 233.

13. Ibid., 214, 213, 222.

14. Ibid., 233.

15. *CWE* 27, 204, 216.

16. E.g. ibid., 227, where he cites Deuteronomy, Ezekiel, Isaiah and Paul alongside Plato.

17. Ibid., 229; Erasmus cites Aristotle for the various kinds of authority, among them king–subject and 'father over children, husband over wife', 231.

18. *Erasmus on Women*, 89.

19. *CWE* 39, 316.

20. Ibid., 264, 267.

21. *Erasmus on Women*, 16.

22. Ex. 20.12 and Matt. 15.4; Matt. 10.35 and 37.

23. *Erasmus on Women*, 95.

24. *CWE* 39, 593–4.

25. *Erasmus on Women*, 214.

26. *Politics*, 4.1ff.

27. *CWE* 27, 231.

28. Ibid., 232.

29. Ibid., 284.

30. See B. Tierney, 'Hierarchy, Consent and the "Western Tradition"', *Political Theory* 15 (1987) 646–52 (quotations on 648–9).

31. *CWE* 27, 284; *CWE* Ep. 288: 91–6.

32. *Utilissima consultatio de bello Turcis inferendo* (Most Useful Advice on the War against the Turks), Basel, 1531.

33. *De amabili concordia ecclesiae* (On the Amiable Concord of the Church), Basel, 1533.

34. He published *Vom Kriege wieder die Türken* in 1528 and *Eine Heerpredigt wider den Türken* in 1529.

35. *Erasmus Reader*, 325–6.

36. Ibid., 316–17.

37. Ibid., 328.

38. *CWE* 27, 55.

39. *Erasmus Reader*, 319–20.

40. *CWE* 27, 309.

41. Ibid., 315, with some changes in wording.

42. Ibid., 316–17.

43. José Shapiro, *Erasmus and our Struggle for Peace* (Boston, MA, 1950). The quotation comes from the dedication on the frontispiece.

44. 'contrived accusations because . . . in my writings I am lavish in my praise of peace and fierce in my hatred of wars' (*Erasmus Reader*, 318).

45. *CWE* 66, 17.

46. *Erasmus Reader*, 319.

47. *CWE* 27, 312.

48. Ibid., 314.

49. LB II 781E, 778F.

50. *CWE* 27, 311.

51. Ibid., 66, 14.

52. Ibid., 42, 5.

53. Cf. Rom. 13.4, Heb. 4.12, 1 Peter 2.13–14, etc.

54. *CWE* 66, 15.

55. Ibid., 16.

56. Ibid., 42, 73. See also ibid., 27, 235.

57. LB V 769–70.

58. ASD V–3, 303.

59. Witzel published his translation under the title *Von der einigkeyt der*

kyrchen. Durch Erasmus von Roterodam ytzt new ausgangen (Erfurt, 1534); Capito's translation was entitled *Von der Kirchen lieblicher Vereinigung und von hinlegung dieser zeit haltenden spaltung in der glauben leer, geschrieben durch den hochgelehrten und weitberiempten Herren Des. Erasmus von Roterdam* (Strasburg, 1533). For other examples of Erasmus's political influence, see J. Estes, '*Officium principis christiani*: Erasmus and the Origins of the Protestant State Church', *ARG* 83 (1992) 66–7.

60. For his praise of Capito in 1516 see *CWE* Ep. 541: 107–9; he stopped corresponding with Capito after 1523. He did not reply to Witzel's two letters (Allen Ep. 2716, Ep. 2786).

61. *Opera Cassandri* (Paris, 1616) 894–5. For references to Vincent of Lérins, see ibid., 1118, Ep. 1123.

CHAPTER 5

1. *CWE* Ep. 181: 6–7.

2. Quoted by J. Lupton, *A Life of John Colet* (London, 1887) 109–10.

3. Ibid., 110–11.

4. *CWE* Ep. 182: 126–39.

5. Ibid., 144–62, 219–22.

6. PL 23, 470B quoted in Erasmus's *Capita contra morosos*, LB VI **4r.

7. *CWE* Ep. 446: 66–9.

8. Ibid., 373: 98–9, 117.

9. Ibid., 55–64.

10. Ibid., 337: 881–906.

11. E. F. Rogers, *The Correspondence of Sir Thomas More* (Princeton, 1947), Ep. 15: 42–3.

12. Jerome at PL 28: 179A, PL 23, 470B quoted by Erasmus in his *Capita contra morosos* LB VI **4r.

13. *CWE* Ep. 182: 136–9; cf. PL 29: 558B –559: 'poorly rendered by bad translators . . . changed by nodding scribes'.

14. *CWE* Ep. 335: 239–42.

15. See above Chapter 2.

16. *Antapologia* (Paris, 1526) 153 recto.

17. See above Chapter 2.

18. Allen Ep. 1920: 19–28.

19. Ibid., 1846: 10–12, 27–9.

20. Ibid., 1814: 150–2.

21. Ibid., 1908: 73–5, 1903: 35–6.

22. LB IX 922E.

23. Ibid., 922C–D.

24. Cf. *CWE* Ep. 1341A: 833–4.

25. Quoted by M. Bataillon, *Erasme et l'Espagne* (Geneva, 1991) 417; Sepúlveda, *Opera omnia* (Madrid, 1780) I, 467–8.

26. *Responsio*, 98 verso.

27. Allen Ep. 2263: 17.

28. Ibid., 2513: 695.

29. *Apologia pro pietate*, ed. J. Coppens (Brussels, 1975) 91.

30. Cf. *CWE* Ep. 1466: 15 and note.

31. *Contra morosos*, LB VI **3 verso; sim. to Béda LB IX 846F and 560E–F.

32. *CWE* 71, 21.

33. Allen Ep. 1301: 26–7.

34. LB IX 985C, 905D.

35. LB VI *** 3 verso.

36. Carranza brought this accusation against Erasmus in his *Apologia de tribus locis* (Rome, 1522), P3 recto–verso. He was referring to Erasmus's annotation at LB VI 855B–E.

37. In the 1516 edition, p. 352; the remark, which gave great offence, was deleted after 1519. For his defence see LB IX 401D, 407F, 413D.

38. LB IX 1046B (1066E).

39. Ibid., 1030B.

40. Ibid., 1037C, 1050A.

41. Ibid., 1082E, 1092A.

42. Allen Ep. 2095: 63–4, 68–9.

43. *Bellaria* (Cologne, 1539) B7 verso.

44. Allen Ep. 2315: 225–34, 300 and Ep. 2932: 28–29.

45. *CWE* 7, 341, 343, 344.

46. Cf. *CWE* Ep. 1165: 14, Ep. 1173: 125, *CWE* 39, 446.

47. *CWE* 40, 836.

48. Ortensio Lando, *In Des. Erasmi funus dialogus lepidissimus* (Basel, 1540) B1 recto–verso.

49. *CWE* Ep. 1352: 37–9.

CHAPTER 6

1. Allen Ep. 1155: 8.

2. Letter of 1523 quoted in E. Rummel, *Confessionalizatuen*, 82.

3. Ms Munich, Bayerische Staatsbibliothek, 'Autograph Cochlaeus', dated 28 May 1520.

4. Amerbachkorrespondenz 2, 320, 477; Beatus Rhenanus, Briefwechsel, 301.

5. Allen Ep. 1342: 603–4 (1523), Klawiter, 225.

6. *CWE* Ep. 933: 4–6.

7. He names Melanchthon and Capito, both of whom could be labelled 'humanists' at the time.

8. Ibid., lines 36–9.

9. His criticism was, however, reported to Erasmus as early as 1516 in a letter from Spalatin, who told him of a certain Augustinian's disapproval of his views on works and on original sin. Cf. *CWE* Ep. 501.

10. Erasmus published the letter only after several unauthorized printings. Because it was a personal communication and rather candid, it caused trouble for Erasmus, who was obliged to explain his meaning in the apologetic *CWE* Ep. 1033.

11. *CWE* Ep. 980 (of 30 May 1519): 8–11.

12. Ibid., 980: 45–54.

13. Ibid., 1033: lines 226–31.

14. Ibid., 1127A: 51–69.

15. Ibid., lines 75–81, 9–7.

16. *CWE* Ep. 1141: 35–6.

17. Ibid., 1202: 326–7, 47, 273–4.
18. Ibid., lines 54–5.
19. Ibid., lines 9–10.
20. Ibid., lines 59, 66–8.
21. Ibid., lines 63–51, similarly in a letter to Spalatin, *CWE* Ep. 1119: 31–46: 'The truth need not always be put forward, and it makes a difference how it is put forward'.
22. *CWE* Ep. 1202: 146–8.
23. Ibid., 1006: 204–5.
24. Ibid., 1202: 323–6.
25. Ibid., lines 75–6, 93–4, 101.
26. *CWE* Ep. 1167: 182–5.
27. Ibid., 1180: 20–21.
28. Ibid., 1259: 10.
29. Ibid., 1324: 14–16.
30. 'You have attacked me and criticized me with some bitterness' (Ep. 1443: 10). Luther was presumably referring to Erasmus's published correspondence in *Epistolae ad diversos* (1521).
31. WA Br III: 96: 15–18.
32. *CWE* Ep. 1443: 15–25, 48–50, 72–8.
33. WA Br II: 499, published by Hans Schott, Strasbourg, January 1523.
34. Ep. 1445.
35. *CWE* Ep. 1496: 183–212.
36. *CWE* 76, 14.
37. Ibid., 7.
38. Ibid., 9.
39. Ibid., 12.
40. Ibid., 18–19. Similarly 233: 'if linguistic skill and common sense are enough for a clear understanding of Scripture, why was there any need in Paul's time for prophets among those who spoke in tongues? Paul distinguishes the gift of tongues from that of prophecy'.
41. Ibid., 20. Similarly 88 ('I do not play the part of a judge here, but of a disputant') and 89 ('I have discussed the issue. Let others pass judgement').

42. Rupp, 106–8.

43. *CWE* 76, 119, 121..

44. Ibid., 121. Compare 139, where he says that 'Christian people have held this doctrine for fifteen hundred years, nor is it right to dispute about it, except in a restrained way and so as to better establish what the church has handed down.'

45. *Ausgewählte Werke*, 161.

46. *CWE* 76, 227.

47. *CWE* 76, 211.

48. Ibid., 222.

49. Ibid., 250, 252.

50. *CWE* 76, 171–4: 1 Cor. 6.1; 2 Phil. 1.18; Eccles. 3.7.

51. Ibid., 177.

EPILOGUE

1. *CWE* Ep. 769: 30–1, 38–9.

2. *Johannes Kesslers Sabbata*, ed. E. Egli and R. Schoch (St Gallen, 1902), 87.

3. *Epistola apologetica . . . pro opere Collationum* (Antwerp, 1530) Ei verso–Eii recto.

4. *WA: Tischreden* I, no. 131; Thomas Lindsay, *History of the Reformation* (New York, 1906) I, 190.

5. L. Jardine, *Erasmus, Man of Letters* (Princeton, 1993) 110–11.

6. B. Mansfield, *Erasmus in the Twentieth Century* (Toronto, 2003) 181.

7. W. Dilthey, *Gesammelte Schriften* (Stuttgart, 1957) II, 74.

8. A. Hartmann and B. Jenny, eds. *Die Amerbachkorrespondenz* (Basel, 1942–) II, 498–9.

9. J. Huizinga, *Erasmus of Rotterdam* (London, 1952) 192.

10. N. Mout, 'Erasmianism in Modern Dutch Historiography', in *Erasmianism: Idea and Reality* (Amsterdam, 1997) 189–98.

11. R. Dahrendorf, 'Erasmus-Menschen', in *Merkur, Deutsche Zeitschrift für europäisches Denken* 11–53 (1999) 1063, 1068.

Select Bibliography

PRIMARY SOURCES (AND ABBREVIATIONS)

Allen	P.S. Allen and H.W. Garrod (eds) *Opus epistolarum Des. Erasmi Roterodami* Oxford 1906–58
ASD	*Opera omnia Desiderii Erasmi Roterodami* Amsterdam 1969–
Ausgewählte Werke	H. Holborn (ed.) *Desiderius Erasmus Roterodamus. Ausgewählte Werke* Munich 1933
CWE	*The Collected Works of Erasmus* Toronto 1974–
Erasmus on Women	E. Rummel (ed.) *Erasmus on Women* Toronto 1996
Erasmus Reader	E. Rummel (ed.) *The Erasmus Reader* Toronto 1990
LB	J. Leclerc (ed.) *Desiderii Erasmi Roterodami Opera omnia* Leiden 1703–6, repr. 1961–2
WA	*D. Martin Luthers Werke: Kritische Gesamtausgabe* (Weimar, 1906–61)

SECONDARY LITERATURE

Collections of essays (and abbreviations)

Colloque Liège	J.-P. Massaut (ed.) *Colloque Erasmien de Liège: Commémoration du 450e anniversaire de la mort d'Erasme* Paris 1987
Colloquia Tours	*Colloquia Erasmiana Turonensia: Douzième stage international d'études humanistes, Tours 1969* 2 vols Paris 1972

Colloquium Mons	*Colloquium Erasmianum: Actes du Colloque International réuni à Mons du 26 au 29 octobre 1967 à l'occasion du cinquième centenaire de la naissance d'Erasme* Mons 1968
El Erasmismo	M. Revuelta Sañudo and C. Morón Arroyo (eds) *El Erasmismo en España* Santander 1986
Erasmianism	Mout, M.E.H.N., H. Smolinsky and J. Trapman (eds) *Erasmianism: Idea and Reality* Amsterdam 1997
Erasmus	T. A. Dorey (ed.) *Erasmus* London 1970
Erasmus of Rotterdam	J. Sperna Weiland and W. Frijhoff (eds) *Erasmus of Rotterdam: The Man and the Scholar* Leiden 1988
Erasmus' Vision	H. Pabel (ed.) *Erasmus' Vision of the Church* Kirksville, MO, 1995
Essays	R. DeMolen (ed.) *Essays on the Works of Erasmus* New Haven, CT/London 1978
PL	J. P. Migne (ed.) *Patrologiae cursus completus . . . series latina* Paris 1844–46.
Scrinium	J. Coppens (ed.) *Scrinium Erasmianum* 2 vols Leiden 1969

Journal abbreviations

ARG	*Archiv für Reformationsgeschichte*
BHR	*Bibliothèque d'humanisme et renaissance*
ERSY	*Erasmus of Rotterdam Society Yearbook*
RQ	*Renaissance Quarterly*
SCJ	*Sixteenth Century Journal*

Monographs and articles

Adams, Robert P. *The Better Part of Valor: More, Erasmus, Colet, and Vives on Humanism, War, and Peace, 1496–1535* Seattle 1962

Asensio, Eugenio 'El erasmismo y las corrientes espirituales afines (Conversos, franciscanos, italianizantes)' *Revista de filologia española* 36 (1952): 31–99

Asso, Cecilia *La Teologia e la Grammatica* Florence 1993

Augustijn, Cornelis 'The Ecclesiology of Erasmus' in *Scrinium* II 135–55

——'Hyperaspistes I: La doctrine d'Erasme et de Luther sur la *Claritas Scripturae*' in *Colloquia Tours* II 737–48

—'Erasmus und die Juden' *Nederlands Archief voor Kerkgeschiedenis* 60 (1980): 22–38

—'Humanisten auf dem Scheideweg zwischen Luther und Erasmus' in O. Pesch (ed.) *Humanismus und Reformation: Martin Luther und Erasmus von Rotterdam in den Konflikten ihrer Zeit* Zürich 1985, 119–34

—*Erasmus, his Life, Works, and Influence* Toronto 1991

—'Verba valent usu: was ist Erasmianismus?' in *Erasmianism* 5–14

Backus, I. 'Erasmus and the Spirituality of the Early Church' in *Erasmus' Vision* 95–114

Backvis, Claude 'La Fortune d'Erasme en Pologne' in *Colloquium Mons* 173–202

Bainton, Roland H. *Erasmus of Christendom* London 1970

Bataillon, Marcel 'Vers une définition de l'érasmisme', in *Colloquia Erasmiana* I 21–34

—*Erasme et l'Espagne*, 2nd French edn, ed. Daniel Devoto 3 vols, Geneva 1991

Bejczy, István *Erasmus and the Middle Ages*, Leiden 2001

Béné, Charles *Erasme et Saint Augustin ou influence de Saint Augustin sur l'humanisme d'Erasme* Geneva 1969

Bentley, Jerry H. *Humanists and Holy Writ: New Testament Scholarship in the Renaissance* Princeton NJ, 1983

Bierlaire, Franz *La familia d'Erasme: Contribution à l'histoire d'humanisme* Paris 1968

—*Erasme et ses Colloques: le livre d'une vie* Geneva 1977

Bietenholz, Peter G. *History and Biography in the Work of Erasmus of Rotterdam* Geneva 1966

—'"Haushalten mit der Wahrheit": Erasmus im Dilemma der Kompromissbereitschaft' *Basler Zeitschrift für Altertumskunde* 86 (1986): 9–26

Born, Lester K. 'Erasmus on Political Ethics: The *Institutio Principis Christiani*' *Political Science Quarterly* 43 (1928): 520–43

Bouyer, Louis *Autour d'Erasme: Etudes sur le christianisme des humanistes catholiques* Paris 1955

Boyle, Marjorie O'Rourke *Erasmus on Language and Method in Theology* Toronto 1977

—*Christening Pagan Mysteries: Erasmus in Pursuit of Wisdom* Toronto 1981

—*Rhetoric and Reform: Erasmus' Civil Dispute with Luther* Cambridge, MA/London 1983

Brachin, Pierre 'Vox clamantis in deserto: Réflexions sur le pacifisme d'Erasme' in Colloquia Tours I 247–75

Bradshaw, Brendan 'The Christian Humanism of Erasmus' Journal of Theological Studies 33 (1982): 411–47

Buck, August (ed.) Erasmus und Europa Wiesbaden 1988

Callahan, Virginia W. 'The De Copia: The Bounteous Horn' in Essays 99–109

Cantimori, Delio 'Erasmo e l'Italia' in Umanesimo e religione nel Rinascimento Turin 1975, 60–87

Carrington, Laurel 'The Boundaries between Text and Reader: Erasmus' Approach to Reading Scripture' ARG 88 (1997): 5–22

Caspari, Fritz 'Erasmus on the Social Functions of Christian Humanism' Journal of the History of Ideas 8 (1947): 78–106

Chantraine, Georges 'L'Apologia ad Latomum. Deux conceptions de théologie,' in Scrinium II 51–75

—— 'Mystère' et 'Philosophie du Christ' selon Erasme Namur/Gembloux 1971

——Erasme et Luther, libre et serf arbitre Paris/Namur 1981

Charlier, Yvonne Erasme et l'amitié d'après sa correspondance Paris 1977

Chomarat, Jacques Grammaire et rhétorique chez Erasme 2 vols, Paris 1981

Christ-von Wedel, Christine Das Nichtwissen bei Erasmus von Rotterdam: Zum philosophischen und theologischen Erkennen in der geistigen Entwicklung eines christlichen Humanisten Basel/Frankfurt a.M. 1981

Coogan, R. Erasmus, Lee and the correction of the Vulgate: The Shaking of the Foundations Geneva 1992

Crahay, Roland 'Les censeurs louvanistes d'Erasme', in Scrinium I 221–49

Crisan, Constantin 'Erasme en Roumanie: Approximations diachroniques et synchroniques' in Colloquia Tours I 175–85

Cytowska, Maria 'Erasme en Pologne avant l'époque du Concile de Trente' Erasmus in English 5 (1972): 10–16

Dahrendorf, R. 'Erasmus-Menschen', in Merkur, Deutsche Zeitschrift für europäisches Denken 11–53 (1999)

Derwa, Marcelle, and Marie Delcourt 'Trois aspects humanistes de l'épicurisme chrétien,' in Colloquium Mons 119–33

Devereux, E.J. Renaissance English Translations of Erasmus: A Bibliography to 1700 Toronto/Buffalo, NY/London 1983

Dickens, A.G. *Erasmus the Reformer* London 1994

Dolan, J. *The Influence of Erasmus, Witzel, and Cassander in the Church Ordinances and Reform Proposals of the United Duchies of Cleve during the Middle Decades of the Sixteenth Century* Münster 1957

Dolfen, Christian *Die Stellung des Erasmus von Rotterdam zur scholastischen Methode* Osnabrück 1936

Douglas, A.E. 'Erasmus as Satirist' in *Erasmus* 31–54

Dresden, S. 'Erasme et la notion de *Humanitas*' in *Scrinium* II 527–45

Ducke, Karl-Heinz *Das Verständnis von Amt und Theologie im Briefwechsel zwischen Hadrian VI. und Erasmus von Rotterdam* Leipzig 1973

Dust, P. *Three Renaissance Pacifists: Essays in the Theories of Erasmus, More, and Vives* New York 1987

Eden, Kathy *Friends Hold All Things in Common: Tradition, Intellectual Property, and the Adages of Erasmus* New Haven, CT/London 2001

Eire, C. *War Against the Idols: The Reformation of Worship from Erasmus to Calvin* Cambridge 1986

Estes, James M. '*Officium principis christiani*: Erasmus and the Origins of the Protestant State Church' *ARG* 83 (1992): 49–72

Etienne, Jacques *Spiritualisme érasmien et théologiens louvanistes: Un changement de problématique au début du XVIe siècle* Louvain 1956

Faludy, George *Erasmus of Rotterdam* London 1970

Farge, James K. *Orthodoxy and Reform in Early Reformation France: The Faculty of Theology in Paris 1500–1543* Leiden 1985

——'Erasmus, the University of Paris, and the Profession of Theology' in *ERSY* 19 (1999):18–46

Fernandez, José A. 'Erasmus on the Just War' *Journal of the History of Ideas* 34 (1973): 209–26

Friesen, A. *Erasmus and the Anabaptists, and the Great Commission* (Grand Rapids, MI, 1998)

Garber, Klaus 'L'Humanisme européen et l'utopie pacifiste: essai de reconstitution historique' in *Colloquium Mons* 393–425

Garin, Eugenio 'Erasmo e l'Umanesimo italiano' *BHR* 33 (1971): 7–17

Gerrish, B.A. '*De Libero Arbitrio* (1524): Erasmus on Piety, Theology, and the Lutheran Dogma' in *Essays* 187–209

Gilmore, Myron P. '*Fides et Eruditio*: Erasmus and the Study of History' in Gilmore (ed.) *Humanists and Jurists: Six Studies in the Renaissance* Cambridge, MA, 1963, 87–114

——'Les Limites de la tolérance dans l'oeuvre polémique d'Erasme' in *Colloquia Tours* II 713–36

——'Italian Reactions to Erasmian Humanism' in Heiko A. Oberman and

Thomas A. Brady, Jr (eds) *Itinerarium Italicum: The Profile of the Italian Renaissance in the Mirror of Its European Transformations* Leiden 1975, 61–115

Glomski, Jacqueline 'Erasmus and Cracow (1510–30)' *ERSY* 17 (1997):1–18

Godin, André 'De Vitrier à Origène: recherches sur la patristique érasmienne' in *Colloquium Mons* 47–57

——*Erasme lecteur d'Origène* Geneva 1982

Gordon, Walter M. *Humanist Play and Belief: The Seriocomic Art of Desiderius Erasmus* Toronto 1990

Grendler, Paul 'How to Get a Degree in Fifteen Days: Erasmus's Doctorate in Theology from the University of Turin' *ERSY* 18 (1998) 40–69

Grendler, Paul and Marcella 'The Survival of Erasmus in Italy' *Erasmus in English* 8 (1976): 2–22

Hägglund, Bengt 'Die Frage der Willensfreiheit in der Auseinandersetzung zwischen Erasmus und Luther' in A. Buck (ed.) *Renaissance–Reformation: Gegensätze und Gemeinsamkeiten* Wiesbaden 1984, 181–95

Halkin, Léon-E. 'Erasme en Italie' in *Colloquia Tours* I 37–53

——*Erasmus ex Erasmo: Erasme éditeur de sa correspondance* Aubel 1983

——'La Piété d'Erasme' *Revue d'histoire ecclésiastique* 79 (1984): 671–708

——*Erasme parmi nous* Paris 1987

——*Erasmus: A Critical Biography* Oxford 1993

Hardin, Richard F. 'The Literary Conventions of Erasmus' *Education of a Christian Prince*: Advice and Aphorism' *RQ* 35 (1982): 151–63

Haverals, Marcel 'Une première Redaction du *De contemptu mundi* d'Erasme dans un Manuscript de Zwolle' *Humanistica Lovaniensia* 30 (1981): 40–54

Headley, John M. 'Gattinara, Erasmus, and the Imperial Configurations of Humanism' *ARG* 71 (1980): 64–98

Heath, Michael J. 'Erasmus and the Infidel' in *ERSY* 16 (1996):19–33

Heesakkers, Chris L. 'Argumentatio a persona in Erasmus's Second Apology against Alberto Pio' in *Erasmus of Rotterdam* 79–87

Hentze, Willi *Kirche und kirchliche Einheit bei Desiderius Erasmus von Rotterdam* Paderborn 1974

Henze, Barbara 'Erasmianisch: Die "Methode", Konflikte zu lösen? Das Wirken Witzels und Cassanders', in *Erasmianism* 155–68

Hoffmann, Manfred *Erkenntnis and Verwirklichung der wahren Theologie nach Erasmus von Rotterdam* Tübingen 1972

——*Rhetoric and Theology: The Hermeneutic of Erasmus* Toronto 1994

Holeczek, Heinz 'Die Haltung des Erasmus zu Luther nach dem Scheitern seiner Vermittlungspolitik 1520/1' ARG 64 (1973): 85–11

——*Humanistische Bibelphilologie als Reformproblem bei Erasmus von Rotterdam, Thomas More und William Tyndale* Leiden 1975

——*Erasmus Deutsch: Die volkssprachliche Rezeption des Erasmus von Rotterdam in der reformatorischen Öffentlichkeit* Stuttgart-Bad Cannstatt 1983

Homza, Lu Ann 'Erasmus as Hero or Heretic? Spanish Humanism and the Valladolid Assembly of 1527' *RQ* 50 (1997): 78–118

Honée, Eugène 'Erasmus und die Religionsverhandlungen der deutschen Reichstage (1524–30)' in *Erasmianism* 65–75

Huerga, Alvaro 'Erasmismo y Alumbradismo' in *El Erasmismo* 339–55

Huizinga, Johan *Erasmus of Rotterdam* London 1952

Hyma, Albert *The Youth of Erasmus* Ann Arbor, MI, 1930

IJsewijn, J. and C. Matheeussen 'Erasme et l'historiographie' in G. Verbeke and J. IJsewijn (eds) *The Late Middle Ages and the Dawn of Humanism outside Italy* The Hague 1972, 31–43

Isnardi-Parente, Margherita 'Erasme, la République de Platon et la communauté des biens' in *Erasmus of Rotterdam* 40–45

Jardine, Lisa *Erasmus, Man of Letters: The Construction of Charisma in Print* Princeton, NJ, 1993

Jarrott, Catherine A.L. 'Erasmus's Annotations and Colet's Commentaries on Paul: A Comparison of Some Theological Themes' in *Essays* 125–44

Jonge, Henk Jan de '*Novum Testamentum a nobis versum*: The Essence of Erasmus' Edition of the New Testament' *Journal of Theological Studies* 35 (1984): 394–413

Junghans, Helmar *Der junge Luther und die Humanisten* Weimar 1984

Kaegi, Werner 'Hutten und Erasmus: Ihre Freundschaft und ihr Streit' in *Historische Vierteljahrsschrift* 22 (1924–25): 200–78, 461–514

Kaiser, Walter *Praisers of Folly: Erasmus, Rabelais, Shakespeare* Cambridge, MA, 1964

Kardos, Tibor 'L'Ésprit d'Erasme en Hongrie,' in *Colloquia Tours* I 187–214

Kaufman, Peter Iver *Augustinian Piety and Catholic Reform: Augustine, Colet, and Erasmus* Macon 1982

Kerlen, Dietrich *Assertio: Die Entwicklung von Luthers theologischem*

Anspruch und der Streit mit Erasmus von Rotterdam Wiesbaden 1976

Kisch, Guido *Erasmus und die Jurisprudenz seiner Zeit: Studien zum humanistischen Rechtsdenken* Basel 1960

——*Erasmus' Stellung zu Juden and Judentum* Tübingen 1969

Kleinhans, Robert G. 'Luther and Erasmus: Another Perspective' *Church History* 39 (1970): 459–69

—— '*Ecclesiastes sive de Ratione Concionandi*' in *Essays* 253–66

Knott, Betty I. 'Erasmus' Working Methods in "De Copia"' in *Erasmus of Rotterdam* 143–50

Koerber, Eberhard von *Die Staatstheorie des Erasmus von Rotterdam* Berlin 1967

Kohls, E.-W. 'Erasmus und die werdende evangelische Bewegung des 16. Jahrhunderts' in *Scrinium* I 203–19

——*Die Theologie des Erasmus* 2 vols, Basel 1966

—— *Die theologische Lebensaufgabe des Erasmus und die oberrheinischen Reformatoren* Stuttgart 1969

—— *Luther oder Erasmus: Luthers Theologie in der Auseinandersetzung mit Erasmus* Basel 1972

Kristeller, Paul Oskar 'Erasmus from an Italian Perspective' *RQ* 23 (1970): 1–14

Krüger, Friedhelm *Humanistische Evangelienauslegung: Desiderius Erasmus von Rotterdam als Ausleger der Evangelien in seinen Paraphrasen* Tübingen 1986

Kushner, Eva 'Erasmus and the Paradox of Subjectivity' in *ERSY* 18 (1998): 1–20

Lienhard, Marc 'Die Radikalen des 16. Jahrhunderts und Erasmus' in *Erasmianism* 91–104

Locher, G.W. 'Zwingli und Erasmus' in *Scrinium* II 325–50

Lohse, Bernhard 'Marginalien zum Streit zwischen Erasmus und Luther' *Luther: Zeitschrift der Luther Gesellschaft* 46 (1975): 5–24

——'Erasmus und die Verhandlungen auf dem Reichstag zu Augsburg 1530,' in H. Immenkötter, et al. (eds) *Im Schatten der Confessio Augustana. Die Religionsverhandlungen des Augsburger Reichstages 1530 im historischen Kontext* Münster 1997, 71–83

Longhurst John E. *Erasmus and the Spanish Inquisition: The Case of Juan de Valdes* Albuquerque 1950

Maeder, K. *Die* Via Media *in der Schweizerischen Reformation: Studien zum Problem der Kontinuitat im Zeitalter der Glaubensspalt* Zürich 1970

Maguire, John B. 'Erasmus' Biographical Masterpiece: *Hieronymi Stri-donensis Vita*' *RQ* 26 (1973): 265–73

Mann, Margaret (Phillips) *Erasme et les débuts de la Réforme française (1517–1536)* Paris 1934 (repr. Geneva 1978)

——'Erasmus and the Classics' in *Erasmus* 1–30

Mansfield, Bruce *Phoenix of his Age: Interpretations of Erasmus c. 1550–1750* Toronto 1979

——*Man on his Own: Interpretations of Erasmus, c. 1750–1920* Toronto 1992

——'The Social Realism of Erasmus: Some Puzzles and Reflections' in *ERSY* 14 (1994): 1–23

——*Erasmus in the Twentieth Century: Interpretations c. 1920–2000* Toronto 2003

Marc'hadour, Germain 'William Tyndale entre Erasme et Luther,' in *Colloquium Mons* 185–98

——'Erasme et John Colet' in *Colloquia Tours* II 761–9

——'Thomas More in Emulation and Defence of Erasmus' in *Erasmus of Rotterdam* 203–14

——'Erasmus as Priest: Holy Orders in his Vision and Practice' in *Erasmus's Vision* 115–49

Margolin, Jean-Claude *Guerre et paix dans la pensée d'Erasme* Paris 1973

——'Erasme et la vérité' in *Colloquium Mons* 135–70

——*Erasme, precepteur de l'Europe* Paris 1995

Markish, Shimon *Erasmus and the Jews* Chicago, IL 1986

Marsh, David 'Erasmus on the Antithesis of Body and Soul' *Journal of the History of Ideas* 37 (1976): 673–88

Massaut, J.-P. 'Erasme, la Sorbonne et la nature de l'Eglise' in *Colloquium Mons* 89–118

——'Erasme et Saint Thomas' in *Colloquia Tours* II 581–611

Maurer, Wilhelm *Das Verhältnis des Staates zur Kirche nach humanisti-scher Anschauung, vornehmlich bei Erasmus* Giessen 1930

——'Melancthons Anteil am Streit zwischen Luther und Erasmus' *ARG* 49 (1958): 89–115

McConica, James Kelsey 'Erasmus and the Grammar of Consent,' in *Scrinium* II 77–99

——*Erasmus* Oxford 1991

——'The English Reception of Erasmus' in *Erasmianism* 37–46

McCutcheon, Elizabeth 'Erasmus's Representation of Women and their Discourses' in *ERSY* 12 (1992): 64–86

McSorley H.J. 'Erasmus and the Primacy of the Roman Pontiff: Between Conciliarism and Papalism' *ARG* 65 (1974): 37–54

Mesnard, Pierre 'L'Expérience politique de Charles-Quint et les enseigne-ments d'Erasme' in Jean Jacquot (ed.) *Fêtes et cérémonies au temps de Charles-Quint* Paris 1960, 45–56

——'Le Caractère d'Erasme' in *Colloquium Mons* 327–32

Michel, Alain 'La Parole et la beauté chez Erasme' in *Colloquium Mons* 3-17

Miller, Clement A. 'Erasmus on Music' *Musical Quarterly* 52 (1966): 332–49

Minnich, Nelson H. 'Erasmus and the Fifth Lateran Council (1512–17)' in *Erasmus of Rotterdam* 46–60

Moeller, Bernd 'Die deutschen Humanisten und die Anfänge der Refor-mation' *Zeitschrift für Kirchengeschichte* 70 (1959): 46–61

Mout, M.E.H.N. 'Erasmianism in Modern Dutch Historiography' in *Erasmianism: Ideas and Reality* Amsterdam 1997

Nauwelaerts, M.A. 'Erasme à Louvain: Ephémérides d'un séjour de 1517 à 1521' in *Scrinium* I 3–24

Nieto, José C. 'Luther's Ghost and Erasmus' Masks in Spain' *BHR* 39 (1977): 33–49

Oberman, Heiko A. *The Roots of Anti-Semitism in the Age of Renaissance and Reformation* Philadelphia, PA, 1984

O'Donnell, Anne M. 'Contemporary Women in the Letters of Erasmus' in *ERSY* 9 (1989): 34–72

Oelrich, K.H. *Der späte Erasmus und die Reformation* Münster 1961

Olin, John C. *Six Essays on Erasmus* New York 1979

——'Erasmus and Saint Jerome: The Close Bond and Its Significance' in *ERSY* 7 (1987) 33–53

——*Erasmus, Utopia, and the Jesuits: Essays on the Outreach of Humanism* New York 1994

O'Malley, John W. 'Erasmus and Luther, Continuity and Discontinuity as Key to their Conflict' *SCJ* 5 (1974): 47–65

——'Erasmus and the History of Sacred Rhetoric: The *Ecclesiastes* of 1535,' in *ERSY* 5 (1985): 1–29

——'Grammar and Rhetoric in the *pietas* of Erasmus's *Journal of Medieval and Renaissance Studies* 18 (1988): 81–98

Pabel, Hilmar M. *Conversing with God: Prayer in Erasmus's Pastoral Writings* Toronto 1997

——'The Peaceful People of Christ: The Irenic Ecclesiology of Erasmus of Rotterdam' in *Erasmus' Vision* 57–93

Padberg, Rudolf 'Pax Erasmiana: Das politische Engagement und die 'politische Theologie' des Erasmus von Rotterdam, in *Scrinium* II 301–12

——'Erasmus contra Augustinum: das Problem des bellum justum in der erasmischen Friedensethik' in *Colloquia Tours* II 279–96

Panofsky, Erwin 'Erasmus and the Visual Arts' *Journal of the Warburg and Courtauld Institutes* 32 (1969): 200–27

Payne, John B. 'Toward the Hermeneutics of Erasmus,' in *Scrinium* II 13–49

——*Erasmus: His Theology of the Sacraments* Richmond, VA 1970

Pendergrass, Jan N. 'Cassander de Colmars, un correspondant d'Erasme' in *Colloquium Mons* 277–91

Pérez, Joseph 'El erasmismo y las corrientes espirituales afines' in *El Erasmismo* 323–38

Peteghem, P.P.J.L. van 'Erasmus' Last Will, the Holy Roman Empire and the Low Countries' in *Erasmus of Rotterdam* 88–97

Pfeiffer, Rudolf 'Erasmus und die Einheit der klassischen und der christlichen Renaissance' *Historisches Jahrbuch* 74 (1955): 175–88

Pigman, G.W, III 'Imitation and the Renaissance Sense of the Past: The Reception of Erasmus' *Ciceronianus*' *Journal of Medieval and Renaissance Studies* 9 (1979): 155–77

Pollet, J.V.M. 'Origine et structure du 'De sarcienda ecclesiae Concordia' (1533) d'Erasme' in *Scrinium* II 183–95

Post, R.R. *The Modern Devotion: Confrontation with Reformation and Humanism* Leiden 1968

Rabil, Albert, Jr *Erasmus and the New Testament: The Mind of a Christian Humanist* San Antonio, TX, 1972

Rademaker, C.S.M. 'Erasmus and the Psalms: His Commentary on Psalm 86 (85)' in *Erasmus of Rotterdam* 187–94

Reese, Alan W. 'Learning Virginity: Erasmus' Ideal of Christian Marriage' *BHR* 57 (1995): 551–67

Renaudet, Augustin *Erasme et l'Italie* Geneva 1954 (2nd edn, Geneva 1998)

Rice, Eugene 'Erasmus and the Religious Tradition' *Journal of the History of Ideas* 11 (1950): 387–411

Rudolph, Günther 'Das sozialökonomische Denken des Erasmus von Rotterdam' *Deutsche Zeitschrift für Philosophie* 17 (1969): 1076–92

Rummel, Erika *Erasmus as a Translator of the Classics* Toronto 1985

——*Erasmus and His Catholic Critics* 2 vols, Nieuwkoop 1989

—— *The Humanist–Scholastic Debate in the Renaissance and the Refor-mation* Cambridge, MA, 1995

—— *The Confessionalization of Humanism in Reformation Germany* New York 2001

Salomon, Albert 'Democracy and Religion in the Work of Erasmus' *Review of Religion* 14 (1950): 227–49

Schätti, Karl *Erasmus von Rotterdam und die Römische Kurie* Basel 1954

Scheible, Heinz 'Melancthon zwischen Luther und Erasmus' in August Buck (ed.) *Renaissance–Reformation: Gegensätze und Gemein-samkeiten* Wiesbaden 1984, 155–80

Schneider, Elisabeth *Das Bild der Frau im Werk des Erasmus von Rotterdam* Basel/Stuttgart 1955

Schoeck, R.J. *Erasmus of Europe* Vol. 1: *The Making of a Humanist 1467–1500*, Vol. 2: *The Prince of Humanists 1501–1536* Edinburgh 1990, 1993

Schottenloher, Otto '*Lex naturae* und *Lex Christi* bei Erasmus' in *Scrinium* II 253–99

——'Erasmus und die *Respublica Christiana*' *Historische Zeitschrift* 210 (1970): 295–323

Screech, M.A. *Ecstasy and the Praise of Folly* London 1980

Scribner, R.W. 'The Social Thought of Erasmus' *Journal of Religious History* 6 (1970): 3–26

——'The Erasmians and the Beginning of the Reformation in Erfurt' *The Journal of Religious History* 9 (1976–77): 3–31

Seidel Menchi, Silvana *Erasmo in Italia 1520–1580* Turin 1987

——'Do We Need the "ism"? Some Mediterranean Perspectives' in *Eras-mianism* 47–64

Shapiro, José, *Erasmus and our Struggle for Peace* Boston, MA 1950

Smith, Preserved *Erasmus: A Study of His Life, Ideals and Place in History* New York/London 1923; repr. New York 1962

Smolinsky, Heribert 'Erasmianismus in der Politik? Das Beispiel der vereinigten Herzogtümer Jülich-Kleve-Berg,' in *Erasmianism* 77–89

Sowards, J.K. *Desiderius Erasmus* Boston 1975

——'Erasmus and the Education of Women' *SCJ* 13 (1982): 77–89

——'Erasmus as a Practical Educational Reformer' in *Erasmus of Rotterdam* 123–31

Stupperich, Robert 'Das *Enchiridion militis christiani* des Erasmus von Rotterdam nach seiner Entstehung, seinem Sinn und Charakter' *ARG* 69 (1978): 5–23

Telle, Emile V. *Erasme de Rotterdam et le septième sacrament: Etude d'é-*

vangélisme matrimonial au XVIe siècle et contribution à la biographie intellectuelle d'Erasme Geneva 1954

——'Dolet et Erasme' in *Colloquia Tours* I 407–39

Thompson, Geraldine *Under Pretext of Praise: Satiric Mode in Erasmus' Fiction* Toronto 1973

Tierney, B. 'Hierarchy, Consent and the "Western Tradition"' *Political Theory* 15 (1987): 646–52

Torrance T.F. 'The Hermeneutics of Erasmus' in Elsie Anne McKee and Brian G. Armstrong *Probing the Reformed Tradition: Historical Studies in Honor of Edward A. Dowey, Jr* Louisville, KY, 1989, 48–76

Torzini, Roberto *I labirinti del Libero Arbitrio: La discussione tra Erasmo e Lutero* Florence 2000

Tracy, James D. *Erasmus: The Growth of a Mind* Geneva 1972

——*The Politics of Erasmus: A Pacifist Intellectual and His Political Milieu* Toronto 1978

——'Erasmus among the Postmodernists: *Dissimulatio, Bonae Literae*, and *Docta Pietas* Revisited' in *Erasmus' Vision* 1–40

——*Erasmus of the Low Countries* Berkeley 1996

Trapman, Johannes ''Erasmianism' in the Early Reformation in the Netherlands' in *Erasmianism* 169–76

——'Erasmus on Lying and Simulation' *Intersections: Yearbook for Early Modern Studies* 2 (2002) 33–46

Trencsényi-Waldapfel, Imre 'L'Humanisme belge et l'humanisme hongrois liés par l'esprit d'Erasme' in *Commémoration nationale d'Erasme* Brussels 1970 209–24

Trinkaus, Charles 'Erasmus, Augustine, and the Nominalists' *ARG* 67 (1976): 5–32

Turchetti, Mario 'Une Question mal posée: Erasme et la tolérance. L'idée de *sygkatabasis*' *BHR* 53 (1991): 379–95

Vogel, C.J. de 'Erasmus and his Attitude towards Church Dogma' in *Scrinium* II 101–32

Vredeveld, Harry 'The Ages of Erasmus and the Year of his Birth' *RQ* 46 (1993): 754–809

Weiler, A.G. 'The Turkish Argument and Christian Piety in Desiderius Erasmus' *Consultatio de Bello Turcis Inferendo* (1530)' in *Erasmus of Rotterdam* 30–39

Weiss, James M. '*Ecclesiastes* and Erasmus: The Mirror and the Image' *ARG* 65 (1974): 83–108

Wengert, T. *Human Freedom, Christian Righteousness: Philip Melanchthon's Exegetical Dispute with Erasmus of Rotterdam* Oxford 1998

Wesseling, Ari 'Are the Dutch Uncivilized? Erasmus on the Batavians and his National Identity' in *ERSY* 13 (1993): 68–102

Williams, George Hunston 'Erasmianism in Poland: An Account of a Major, though Ever Diminishing, Current in Sixteenth-Century Polish Humanism and Religion, 1518-1605' *Polish Review* 22 (1977): 3–50

Williams, Kathleen (ed.) *Twentieth-Century Interpretations of* The Praise of Folly: *A Collection of Critical Essays* Englewood Cliffs, NJ, 1969

Winkler, Gerhard B. *Erasmus von Rotterdam und die Einleitungsschriften zum Neuen Testament: Formale Strukturen und theologischer Sinn* Münster 1974

Wollgast, Siegfried 'Erasmianer und die Geschichte des Nonkonformismus. Aspekte' in *Erasmianism* 105–26

Woodward, William *Desiderius Erasmus Concerning the Aim and Method of Education* New York 1964

Zambelli, P. 'Corneille Agrippa, Erasme et la Théologie Humaniste' in *Colloquia Tours* II 113–59

Index